What's a Schwa Sound Anyway?

———

A Holistic Guide to Phonetics,
Phonics, and Spelling

———

Sandra Wilde

Heinemann
Portsmouth, NH

Heinemann
A division of Reed Elsevier Inc.
361 Hanover Street
Portsmouth, NH 03801-3912
Offices and agents throughout the world

Library of Congress Cataloging-in-Publication Data

Wilde, Sandra.
What's a schwa sound anyway? : a holistic guide to phonetics,
phonics, and spelling / by Sandra Wilde.
p.   cm.
Includes bibliographical references and index.
ISBN 0-435-08865-3 (alk. paper)
1. Reading—Phonetic method—United States.   2. English language—
Orthography and spelling.   I. Title.
LB1050.34.W4383   1997
372.6—dc21   97-602
                                                                CIP

Editors: Toby Gordon and Scott Mahler
Copy Editor: Alan Huisman
Production Editor: Renée M. Nicholls
Cover Designer: Michael Leary
Manufacturing Coordinator: Louise Richardson

Printed in the United States of America on acid-free paper

06   VP   9

*To Yetta and Ken Goodman,
who continue to teach me so
much of what I know about
literacy*

Contents

Contents

Acknowledgments

I'd like to give a special thank you to Toby Gordon, who was my editor at Heinemann from the time I signed my first book contract in 1989 until her recent departure. I miss you, Toby! I also thank Scott Mahler, who took over as editor of this book, for his interest and support. Further thanks go to Alan Huisman for his (as always!) brilliant copy editing, Renée Nicholls as production editor, and Michael Leary for the cover design. The work of Mike Gibbons, Sheila Peters Baston, Susie Stroud, Karen Hiller, Cherie Lebel, and others in getting my work out to readers is always much appreciated. David Freeman and Steve Bialostok were intelligent readers of the manuscript; their comments provoked important revisions.

At Portland State University, I'd like to thank Christine Chaillé, Emily de la Cruz, Donna Shrier, and Linda Darling. Valerie Chapman, Leanne Kerner, and other members of St. Francis of Assisi have helped me keep my life in balance. I am thankful for Lois Bridges, who has been a sounding board on phonics and lots of other issues. Special gratitude and appreciation go to Bill Kruger.

Introduction

The dreadful schwa, bane of the basal reader phonics lesson!

To many of us who are now whole language teachers but began our careers when basal readers were used in most elementary school classrooms, the schwa was part of what led us to whole language in the first place. We didn't understand this linguistic terminology ourselves, so how could we teach it to kids? And some of us wondered (subversively), *Should* we teach it to kids? Were six-year-olds who could talk about glided and unglided vowels better readers than those who couldn't? (And if they were, which was cause and which was effect?)

Classrooms have changed, and the debates have shifted ground somewhat, but many teachers still find themselves wondering about letters and sounds and phonics. What role does phonics play in learning to read? Does it still have a place in classrooms where children are becoming literate through rich experiences with literature and writing? Why have the debates about phonics continued and in some ways grown more heated? What *is* a schwa sound anyway? And who cares?

This book addresses these questions and many others related to phonics and its relationship to learning to read and spell. My first goal is to increase your background knowledge, and thus the book in some sense is an introduction to the phonetics, phonology, and orthography of English (terms I define later). In the old days, textbooks on these topics were often used in teacher education courses to help beginning teachers understand basal reader phonics lessons. But my motivation is very different: I want to help teachers think intelligently about the role of letter-sound relationships in learning to read and spell, as well as look at students' miscues and invented spellings with as sophisticated an understanding as possible.

Here's an example: a first grader spells the word *went* as WET. (I'm using the convention of uppercase letters for invented spellings.) A typical reaction to this spelling would be that the child is having trouble hearing *n* sounds. Instructionally, we might then think that the child should at least be told to listen carefully for all the sounds in the word and perhaps be given some extra practice on *n*. But a teacher with some linguistic background will realize that when a sound like *n* comes before another consonant sound, it's often more "weakly" pronounced, so that young children may leave it out of their spelling. What this child is doing is absolutely normal!

One of the most liberating effects of linguistic knowledge is knowing how to tell the pathological from the normal and realizing that much of what looks unusual or problematic in a child's reading or writing really isn't.

This book is divided into two sections, the first half intended to build your linguistic knowledge base and the second to help you apply it.

The first four chapters discuss the basic building blocks of written language and are presented as responses to questions: questions teachers often ask about phonics, and questions they didn't know they had. Chapter 1 deals with the sounds of English and Chapters 2 and 3 take on the not-so-simple relationships between sounds and letters that we use when we read and spell. As I'm only too aware that even mentioning the topic of linguistics strikes fear (or boredom) in the hearts of many, I've done everything possible to make this material user-friendly (short sections, lots of examples, and, I hope, some humor). Chapter 4 is then devoted to issues of language variation, for two reasons. First, it further illustrates that phonics isn't a simple matter of learning the sounds that letters stand for. Second, so many of our citizens are still stigmatized because of their speech, and I believe deeply that teachers have a responsibility to challenge such judgments.

The chapters in the second section show you how powerful linguistic knowledge can be. Chapter 5 deals with general issues related to how children should learn about letter-sound relationships and the role such knowledge plays in reading and spelling. I haven't tried to do a complete how-to for helping children learn about phonics and spelling (but see K. Goodman 1993 and Mills, O'Keefe & Stephens 1992 for phonics, and Wilde 1992 for spelling) but rather to suggest ways of thinking about many of the instructional issues. Chapters 6 and 7 then focus on kidwatching with a sophisticated eye: looking at children's invented spellings and miscues, respectively, to see what their evolving use of letter-sound relationships can teach us about who and where they are as learners. This is, of course, what it's ultimately all about: using our knowledge of language and learning to become better teachers of the children we work with.

So what's a schwa sound anyway, and why should I care? The schwa is a weak mid-central vowel sound in English that occurs in unaccented syllables, symbolized by the funny little upside-down e (ə) that you've probably noticed in dictionaries. Some words in which it appears are the first syllables of *about* and *upon* and the middle syllable of *medicine* (when these words are pronounced the way they are in normal speech; try saying them in a sentence with normal inflection).

Why might it be useful for teachers to know this? Because of all the vowel sounds, the schwa is the most likely to be misspelled, since its spelling is related not to pronunciation but the word's origin. (We sometimes see this by looking at a related word; for instance, the vowel pronounced as a schwa in *medicine* is pronounced as a short *i* in *medicinal*.) In doing research for my dissertation (Wilde, 1986/1987), which is a study of the spelling of six third and fourth graders, I discovered that although the children spelled vowel sounds correctly 93 percent of the time, they spelled the schwa sound correctly only 82 percent of the time (i.e., the schwa was misspelled two and a half times as often as vowels in general—18 percent versus 7 percent of the time).

What does this mean for instruction? Spelling *esophagus* as ESOFIGIS doesn't mean that the writer has a problem with two different vowel sounds: both the ones she got wrong are schwas, which are hard to spell because you can't "hear" which letter to use. Phonics is of no help here! But we can tell kids that if they can't tell clearly what sound they hear in a word, they should probably check it in the dictionary or elsewhere if they want to get it right. (More on all this later.)

I hope I've justified the title of the book and intrigued you enough to keep reading. The book is meant to be read in order, since the second half assumes you know the material in the first half. If you get bogged down by the level of linguistic detail you may want to skip ahead and come back. But please don't be afraid of the linguistics in the first half of the book; now more than ever, teachers who choose not to use formal, structured programs in phonics and spelling need to make it clear that we realize that letter-sound relationships are an important cueing system of written language. Even more important, informed teachers are stronger kidwatchers and teach in ways that are more responsive to children's development. Let's prove that a child-centered, whole language teacher who knows a lot about phonics isn't an oxymoron!

Part One

ONE

The Sounds of English

Welcome to the world of phonics, where your guide from the Whole Language Travel Bureau will take you on a journey through Vowel Land and Consonant Country, past the twin mountains of Digraph and Diphthong, through the eerie Kingdom of Silent Letters. . . . Okay, I know phonics isn't going to be a new attraction at Disneyland any time soon, but let's spend some time learning about sounds and letters, how they work in our alphabetic spelling system, and how teachers can use this knowledge.

How Much Do Teachers Need to Know About Linguistics?

This may seem like an irrelevant question, because linguistics—the formal study of language and how it works—isn't traditionally part of teacher preparation. Yet consider an analogy to teaching mathematics. Without a solid understanding of mathematical thinking and concepts, it's hard for an elementary school teacher to help children understand mathematics other than as a rote series of procedures. This doesn't mean that elementary teachers should be taking college courses in calculus and analytic geometry, but they

---

I haven't cited specific references for much of the material in this chapter because it's pretty basic and widely known linguistics, but I used Fromkin and Rodman (1993), Kreidler (1989), and Ladefoged (1982) to refresh my memory and check details. When these sources described matters in slightly different ways, I chose an explanation that seemed most accessible.

really do need to understand concepts like place value, base ten, the metric system, and so on, and are often asked to take courses with a focus on "mathematics for teachers" as part of their professional training.

Literacy takes up a large part of the day in most elementary school classrooms, yet usually the only academic preparation in the *content* of literacy (as opposed to teaching methodology) is a course in children's literature. Linguistics has in the past been left to the assumed "experts"—typically the authors of basal readers and spelling textbooks. But, as always, knowledge is power. The teacher with some knowledge of linguistics can be a far better kidwatcher, as well as be able to participate more learnedly in conversations and debates about teaching methodology.

In my ideal world, all prospective elementary school teachers would take an introductory linguistics course focused on material that would be especially valuable for literacy educators to know, exploring not only phonetics, phonology, and phonics but syntax, semantics, and sociolinguistics. The piece of it I'm trying to carve out here isn't the kind of introduction a linguistics major would get; for instance, in the phonetics course I took in graduate school, we learned to produce, identify, and represent with symbols all of the sounds produced in all of the languages of the world. What we will do here instead is focus just on the sounds of English and the way they're represented by our spelling system.

This linguistic information is still fairly complex, but all of it is relevant for teachers, since it increases their sophistication in looking at children's language use. A teacher who is positively disposed toward invented spelling can look at a spelling like OWT for *out* and say, "He made a good guess," but a teacher with stronger linguistic knowledge can say, "He used a spelling for the /au/ phoneme that usually occurs in another linguistic environment [i.e., at the end of a syllable]; this shows me that he knows a lot about how to spell this sound and is just missing one little piece of knowledge. I think I'll keep an eye on how he spells this sound in his future writing."

What's the Difference Between Phonetics, Phonics, and Spelling?

Let's begin by defining some terms. (Here and elsewhere I'm going to be as nontechnical as I can in my definitions and descriptions, trying to be as accurate as possible without being tedious. I'll also use the linguistic convention of representing phonemes, including broad phonetic spellings of words, between slashes, and putting detailed phonetic transcriptions in brackets.) *Phonetics* is the study of speech sounds. For instance, a study of the phonetics of English would consist of describing all the sounds of English in all their variations. An example: in English, the phoneme /t/ has two slightly different sounds, as found in the words *top*, where there's a slight puff of air after the /t/ (represented symbolically as [tʰ]), and *stop*, where there's not. (Actually, there are more than two, but these are the most obvious and best known.) A related area of study, *phonology*, works to explain these variations. For our purposes, it's most useful to think of phonetics as referring to the *sounds* of language.

Phonics is often understood to be a specific teaching method, but its underlying meaning is the relationships between the sounds of language and the letters used to represent them. In phonics as a teaching method, these associations are formally emphasized, but every proficient reader of an alphabetic language has and uses knowledge about phonics. Debates carried on by the general public, however, often underestimate the complexity of this knowledge: "Just teach them which letters go with which sounds and they're all set." If only it were that simple! In a classic study in 1929, Ernest Horn found that there are eighteen sounds associated with the letter *a* alone (by itself or in combination with other vowel letters) in materials that a typical first grader was likely to read (e.g., April, apple, any, was, father, and call, just in words where *a* appears alone).

Orthography is the spelling system of a language. For instance, one feature of the orthography of English is that we use twenty-six letters, another is that we use doubled consonant letters to represent vowel differences between words (as in *robed* and *robbed*). We may talk about readers using phonics knowledge and spellers using orthographic knowledge, but both terms refer to largely the same body of information.

What's a Phoneme?

This is a question you probably didn't know you had, but phonemes are the basic building blocks involved in producing and hearing speech, so we'll need to start with a good understanding of what they are. To make it clear when we're talking about the sounds of a word rather than the word itself or the way it's spelled, the convention is to represent sounds (phonemes) with symbols placed between slashes. Regular alphabet letters are often used, particularly for consonants, but, unlike regular spellings of words, each symbol always represents the same sound.

A *phoneme* can be defined as a single sound that distinguishes one word from another for speakers of a language. For instance, bat (/bæt/) and cat (/kæt/) differ from each other by one phoneme (/b/ in *bat* is replaced by /k/ in *cat*). *Bat* and *bit* (/bɪt/) also differ by one phoneme (the middle one), as do *bat* and *bad* (/bæd/), where the final phoneme changes. In all three cases, the phonetic (technically, phonemic) spellings inside the slashes make this one-phoneme difference easy to see.

Literate adults can find it difficult at first to identify how many phonemes a word has and what they are because our knowledge of a word's spelling can get in the way. For instance, *bat* and *bought* (/bɔt/) also differ by only one phoneme even though the middle sound of *bought* takes four letters to spell.

The phoneme is an abstract, psychological unit rather than a phonetic one, since the same phoneme can be pronounced slightly differently from one word to another or one speaker to another. For instance, the vowel sound in *bag* tends to be slightly different from the one in *bat* (say them and see whether you can hear the difference), but we recognize them as the same phoneme. If you were to make the /æ/ in *bat* a little more "drawn out" like the one in *bag*, it would just sound like you were saying it differently, not like a different word. Change it to /ɪ/, however, and you do have a different word (*bit*).

6

Why Bother with Those Hard-to-Read Phonetic Symbols?

Most of us have some familiarity with phonetic symbols from dictionary pronunciation guides. Some of them are pretty obvious, while others, especially for vowels, are a little more confusing. The International Phonetic Alphabet has conventionalized symbols for every sound of every language in the world, and many teachers may be familiar with a different set of symbols, such as *ā* for the vowel sound in *rain* and *ă* for the vowel sound in *ran*. (These are often used in basal readers and dictionaries.)

Linguists need comprehensiveness and precision, while the layperson is likely to work best with a system that's easily understandable. For this book, I've used some of both systems: IPA symbols in most cases, but with some changes when it seemed that the IPA symbol might be unnecessarily confusing to readers who are more used to dictionary symbols. I've also, whenever possible, represented each phoneme with a single letter or symbol. (There are only two diphthong vowel sounds for which, for reasons of convention, I couldn't do this.) The table I've provided in the appendix shows, for each phoneme, the symbol I've used, a word in which the phoneme appears, and the IPA symbol.

What's the Difference Between a Vowel and a Consonant?

The vowels are *a, e, i, o, u,* and sometimes *y*, right? Unfortunately, no. It's nowhere near that simple. Although those six letters are the ones most often used to represent vowel sounds, the core definition of the term *vowel* refers to sounds, not letters. A vowel sound is one in which air flows through the mouth unobstructed, while a consonant sound is one in which the flow of air is cut off partially or completely. An easy way to feel the difference is to say *ah* (/o/), a vowel sound, and *ssss* (/s/), a consonant sound. It's the way your tongue partially blocks off the stream of breath that produces the hiss of *ssss*.

We'll explore the specifics of vowels and consonants later. But one more thing about vowels and consonants as sounds and as letters. In everyday speech we do talk about vowel (or consonant) letters, but this is really shorthand for letters that usually represent vowel (or consonant) sounds. It's very easy to get this confused when we see a word like *bought*, where the two vowel letters *o* and *u* and the two consonant letters *g* and *h*, are used to represent a single vowel sound. Also, in *quit* /kwɪt/, a vowel letter, *u*, is used to represent the consonant sound /w/, the same sound we hear at the beginning of wit /wɪt/.

What Are the Consonant Sounds of English?

Consonants obstruct the stream of breath to greater and lesser degrees and are therefore divided into five groups: glides, liquids, nasals, fricatives (including the affricate subgroup), and stops. A glide, such as the *y* at the beginning of *yes*, is almost like a vowel. At the other end of the spectrum, the stream of breath is completely closed off for a stop like the *b* at the beginning of *bet*. In fact, if you try to say a /b/ with no following vowel, you can't! You're stuck with the breath trapped behind your closed lips.

In spite of the many groupings, consonants are relatively easy to understand. Teachers for the most part know what the consonant sounds of English are, although some of the information about the relationships between consonant sounds is likely to be new to you and perhaps surprising in what it can reveal about children's linguistic knowledge and processing.

We tend to think of the consonants in alphabetical order: first there's *b*, then *c*, then *d*, and so on. But it's far more informative to think about them categorically.

Stops

As suggested earlier, a *stop consonant* is formed by completely closing off the stream of breath. We can't produce or hear stops in isolation, only in combination with a vowel, so it's not accurate to refer to the /bə/ sound when talking about /b/; it's better to say "the sound we hear at the beginning of *bed*."

Starting at the front of the mouth, there are two stops we make by closing our lips and letting a little air pressure build up behind them: /b/ and /p/. If you get your mouth in position to say *big* and then in position to say *pig*, it feels the same for both. What's different, then? Why and how do these come out as two different words? It has to do with something going on in a very different part of the vocal system: the vocal cords (voice box) in your throat. When you say *big*, your vocal cords vibrate from the beginning of the word, while for *pig*, they don't start vibrating until the vowel is fully underway. You can feel the difference by putting your hand on your throat as you say the two words. (It can be hard to hear the difference with stops, which are quite short. It's a little easier to perceive these two types of sounds if you say *zzzzz*, in which the vocal cords vibrate, and *sssss*, in which they don't.) The linguistic term for this difference is that /b/ and other sounds in which the vocal cords vibrate are *voiced* and /p/ and others without vocal cord vibration are *unvoiced*. This is a major category for describing the consonant sounds of English.

Being able to see and understand the relationships of sounds to each other helps us understand how children use those sounds as they become literate. Consider Jason's piece (Figure 1–1), which reads, "Your rib cage protects your heart. Your liver makes bile. The liver dissolves poison. The liver has vitamins and minerals." In his invented spelling of *protects*, Jason starts the word with *b*. Knowing the phonetic relationship between /p/ and /b/ immediately illuminates the probable reason for this spelling; although he didn't spell the sound that occurs in the word, he spelled one that was extremely close phonetically. And when children are trying to figure out how to spell a word, they often overarticulate it, drawing out the sound. It's easy for sounds to change slightly when their pronunciation is exaggerated.

There are four other stop consonants in English. Moving back a little further in the mouth, /t/ and /d/ are formed with the tongue up on the roof of the mouth, near the front. (The location is most often the small bony ridge right above the front teeth, which is called the *alveolar ridge*.) Can you tell which one is voiced and which is unvoiced? Further back still, with the back of the tongue touching the soft palate (*velum*) at the upper back of the mouth, are /k/ (unvoiced) and /g/ (voiced).

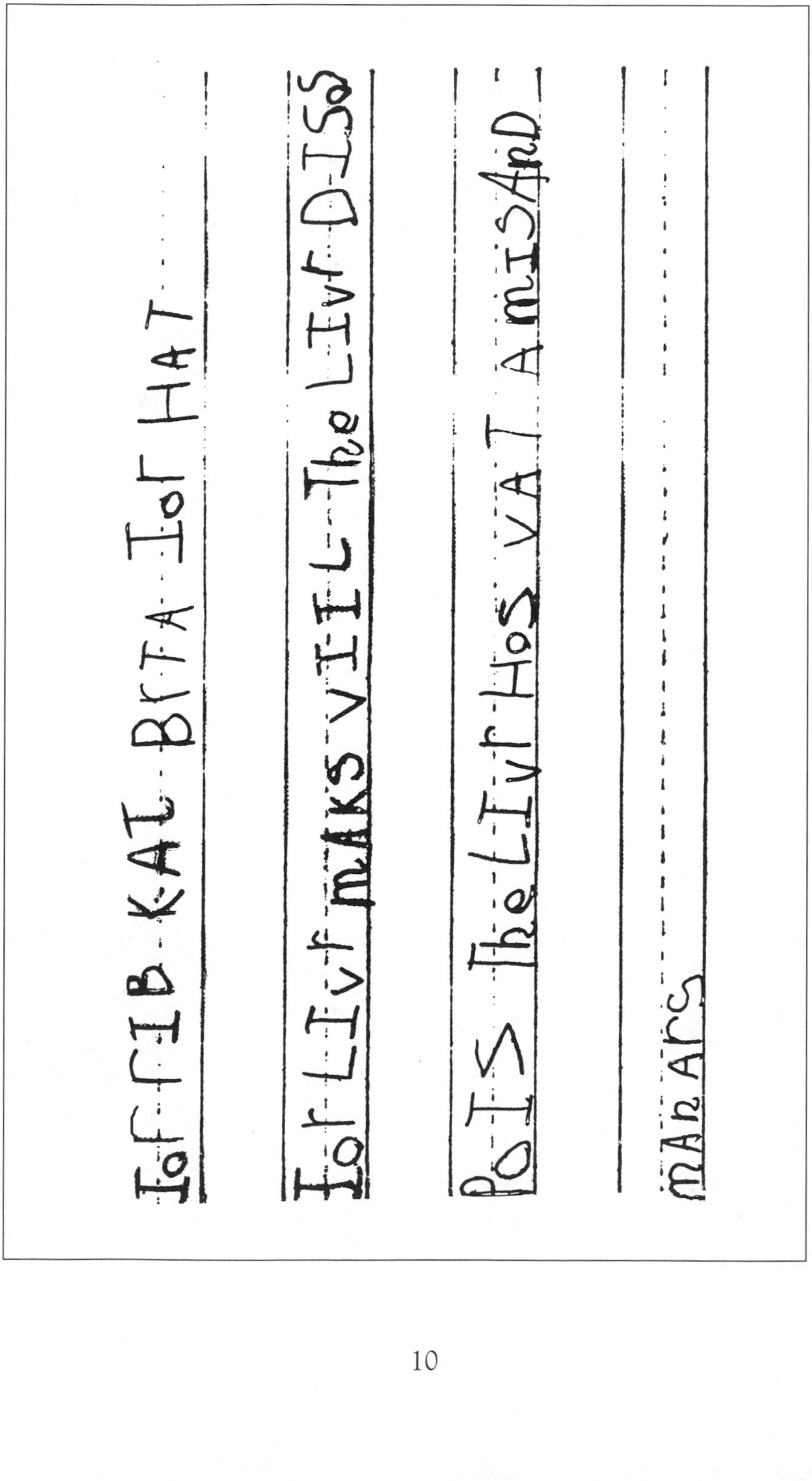

IoF riB KAL BrtA IoF HAT

IoF Livf mAks viiL The Livf DISS

PoIS TheLIvf HoS vAT a misArd

mAh Ars

FIG 1–1 *Jason's piece: "Your rib cage"*

What may have looked like a random list of six consonant sounds can be seen in a paradigm that shows the relationships between them:

Stops

	voiced	unvoiced
lips (bilabial)	/b/	/p/
front of mouth (alveolar)	/d/	/t/
back of mouth (velar)	/g/	/k/

There's one final stop consonant that occurs in English even though it's not a phoneme. It's called the *glottal stop*, and it's created by closing off the stream of air at the vocal cords. What does it sound like? Imagine you're watching a suspense movie and the bad guy has just found a way to break into the unsuspecting victim's house. "Uh-oh!," you say. (Try saying it out loud in an exaggerated way.) The glottal stop is the "catch in the throat" between the *uh* and the *oh*. The symbol for it is /ʔ/. In some English dialects, including several associated with the New York City area, the glottal stop occurs instead of /t/ in some contexts, like the word *bottle*. Since there's no spelling for /ʔ/ and it isn't a phoneme in English, most people aren't very aware of it.

Fricatives

The name *fricatives* reflects how they're created—by friction in the mouth rather than a complete stopping of all breath. Four of them are produced right up at the front of the mouth and involve the teeth: /f/ and /v/, which are called *labiodental* because the lower lip (labio-) is touching the upper teeth (dental); and two *th* sounds that are called dental because the tongue goes between the teeth. Two *th* sounds? Yes; there are both a voiced and an unvoiced *th* sound in English, but many adults don't realize this, because they're spelled the same. We hear the voiced one in *thy* and the unvoiced one in *thigh*. I'll be using the standard IPA symbols for them, /ð/ for the voiced sound that occurs most often in function words like *the*, *this*, and *they*, and /θ/ for the unvoiced sound we usually hear in content words like *think*, *throw*, and *thunder*. (Sometimes, in order to avoid unfamiliar phonetic symbols, dictionaries use *th* for the unvoiced phoneme and *TH* or *th* for the voiced one.)

It can be hard for adults to conceptualize the difference between /ð/ and /θ/ since we're not used to making a distinction between them for spelling purposes. Voiced and unvoiced fricatives are pretty easy to tell apart, though, since they can be drawn out in a way that stops can't. If you say *thy* and *thigh* several times with the *th* part exaggerated, you'll get more of a feel for the phonetic difference.

Moving back in the mouth, there are two pairs of fricatives that occur close together on the roof of the mouth. At the alveolar ridge, close to where /t/ and /d/ are formed, we produce /s/ as in *sip* (unvoiced) and /z/ as in *zip* (voiced). A little further back, at the *palate* (the hard roof of the mouth), we produce the sounds that we hear at the beginning of *ship* (/š/) and at the *z* of azure (/ž/). (These are also sometimes symbolized by *sh* and *zh*.) You may be surprised to find that these are phonemes. Although /š/ is usually spelled with the two letters *sh*, it is indeed a single sound. (More specifically, it's certainly not a combination of the sounds usually made by *s* and *h*.) You may not have even been aware of the /ž/ sound, because it doesn't occur at the beginning of words in English (except in a few words borrowed from other languages like *genre*) and it's spelled a number of different ways, as in *azure, genre, vision, bijou,* and *equation*.

We've now covered fourteen of the consonants of English, and we can put the eight fricatives into a paradigm just like we did the stops:

Fricatives

	voiced	unvoiced
lips and teeth (labiodental)	/v/	/f/
teeth (dental)	/ð/	/θ/
front of mouth (alveolar)	/z/	/s/
roof of mouth (palatal)	/ž/	/š/

Remember Jason's piece where he mentioned that the liver makes bile, which he spelled VIIL (Figure 1–1)? If you compare /b/, a voiced bilabial stop, with /v/, a voiced labiodental fricative, you can see that the sound whose letter he used is pretty close phonetically and physically to the sound that actually occurs in the word. Particularly for an unfamiliar word like this one, it's easy to mishear or misarticulate one of the sounds in it; Jason's spelling is clearly reasonable rather than random.

Affricates

Before we move on to nasals, there are two more consonants that we need to consider along with the fricatives: the sounds we hear at the beginning of *chill* (/č/) and *Jill* (/ɟ/). Can you feel how these sounds are sort of like stops, since your breath is closed off at the beginning of them, yet also sort of like fricatives, since there's some friction before the vowel starts? Phonetically, these two sounds, which are categorized as affricates, are actually a sequence of a stop followed by a fricative, rather than being single sounds. However, for our purposes, and following the practice of many linguists, we'll treat them as single phonemes, since that's how they operate in English. (For instance, they can occur at any position in a word.)

Can you tell which sequence of stop and fricative each of these is a blend of? Here's a clue: if you say *pit sure*, it sounds a lot like *pitcher*. The /č/ sound is indeed a combination of /t/ and /š/; if you substitute the voiced equivalents of these two sounds, /d/ and /ž/, you get /ɟ/. If you break the word *badger* into two syllables, *bad* and *zher*, you get a feel for how the two sounds combine to produce what we hear as /ɟ/. These two affricates are considered palatal because that's the region in the mouth where they end up.

Nasals

Get your mouth ready to say the word *bat*, start to say it, but then instead of opening your mouth, vibrate your vocal cords while pushing some air out your nose. Did it come out as *mat*? (If not, my directions were too confusing! You can get the same effect by getting ready to say *bat* and saying *mat* instead.) The /m/ phoneme is one of three *nasal* sounds in English, which are produced when the mouth is closed off but air goes out the nose instead. (Since no air is getting out of the mouth, some linguists call these sounds *nasal stops*, but calling them *nasals* is less confusing.)

Just as /m/ occurs at the same place of articulation (i.e., location in the mouth) as /b/ and /p/, the second, alveolar, nasal phoneme, /n/, occurs when you start to say *toe* or *dough* but let the air go out your nose instead.

The third nasal sound may be harder to recognize, because it's another one of those phonemes that's written with two letters, and also because it doesn't occur at the beginning of words in English. The nasal sound with the same place of articulation as /k/ and /g/ is /ŋ/, which is the sound we hear at the end of *sing*. This sound isn't a blend of /n/ and /g/, although it's nasal like /n/ and occurs at the back of the mouth like /g/. To further confuse things, /ŋ/ is spelled with just an n in words like *sink*. *Sink* is like *sing* with a /k/ added on, not like *sin* with an added /k/. (Try saying both and you'll hear the difference.) Also, we do have some words in which /ŋ/, even though it doesn't include a /g/ sound itself, is followed by a /g/ sound, as in *anger*.

Children's invented spellings of /ŋ/ are sometimes a wonderful example of how they represent linguistic detail that adults, with our knowledge of standard spellings, no longer notice. Two that I've seen are the spellings FRANGKE for *Frankie* and THINGK for *think*. In each case the child recognized that the word contained the phoneme /ŋ/, which he had presumably learned to spell as *ng* from words like *thing*. (In fact, phonetically, *think* is *thing* plus a /k/ (/θɪŋk/), which the child's spelling represents very accurately!)

If we take our earlier table laying out the stops in relation to each other, we can update it with a column for the nasals:

Stops and Nasals

	voiced	unvoiced	nasal
lips (bilabial)	/b/	/p/	/m/
front of mouth (alveolar)	/d/	/t/	/n/
back of mouth (velar)	/g/	/k/	/ŋ/

Liquids and Glides

The remaining five consonant sounds, two *liquids* and three *glides*, are increasingly similar to vowels. Liquids are sounds in which the airstream is somewhat interrupted but with no real friction; the two liquids of English are /l/ as in *lap* and /r/ as in *rap*. It's hard to define precisely how they're produced, since they vary from speaker to speaker, but /l/ is generally made with the sides of the tongue curled in, while for /r/ the tongue may be bunched up or the tip curled back. Some other languages have an *r* sound that's quite different from the English one; in French, it's often an *uvular trill* (which means that the little thing that hangs down in the back of your throat vibrates). Spanish has two *r* sounds, a light tap against the roof of the mouth as in *pero* and a trill as in *perro*.

The three glides are sometimes called semivowels because they're so much like vowels, but they can't stand on their own like vowels and in English occur mainly followed by vowels. Let's look first at /w/ as in *wet* and /y/ as in *yet*. In both *wet* and *yet*, we move the mouth from one vowellike position to another. Phonetically, /w/ is close to the /u/ of *ooze*, while /y/ is like the /ē/ of *eat*. Slowed down and made into two syllables, *wet* and *yet* come out sounding like *oo-et* and *ee-et* respectively. Sometimes glided vowels (to be defined later) in the middle of words can come out sounding like /w/ or /y/; even though we don't usually spell them that way, children might. In one of my favorite invented spellings, VEASYARE for VCR, it's easy to hear the /y/-like glide if you say the word slowly (vee-see-yar). To further confuse things, the letters *w* and *y* often appear as part of vowel spellings in words like *cow* and *boy*, but in this context these letters are part of the vowel spelling rather than representing consonant glides.

The one consonant sound we haven't yet addressed is the glide /h/, which is produced by forcing air through nonvibrating vocal cords. (It's therefore phonetically closer to the glottal stop than to any other sound, and some linguists classify it as a *glottal fricative*.) In practice, it serves as the voiceless (i.e., whispered) version of the vowel that follows it.

You might be wondering about *wh*, since we've been talking

about /w/ and /h/. For some speakers of English, the beginnings of the words *which* and *witch* are pronounced differently, although this distinction appears to be dropping out of American English. (Even if you make this distinction, there's a good chance that your students don't.) What some speakers produce at the beginning of *which* is a blend of two glides, /w/ and /h/, but in the reverse order of the way it's spelled; phonetically the word is pronounced /hwɪč/.

Before we move on to vowels, let's reflect on our learning. We now know that

- English has twenty-four consonant sounds;
- we can categorize these consonants into five major groups having to do with how they're pronounced (technically speaking, their manner of articulation), each with its own characteristics (six stops, eight fricatives, three nasals, two liquids, and three glides, plus the two affricates, which are a blend of sounds from two groups); and
- we can further classify consonants by place of articulation (where they occur in the mouth), as well as whether they're voiced or not.

Also, we've probably started to suspect that the relationship between the sounds of English and the way we spell them isn't simple. We have some single sounds that take two letters to spell, like the first sound of *ship*, some single letters that really spell a sequence of two sounds, like the *j* of *jig*, and some sets of letters that spell two different sounds, like the *th*'s of *this* and *thick* (to say nothing of the *th* of *fathead!*). And what about the letter *c*? Why do we even need it when we have *s* and *k*? More on these matters later.

What Are the Vowel Sounds of English?

Maybe you think this part will be easy, because we're used to thinking there are only five vowels (*a, e, i, o,* and *u*). However, English has about sixteen different vowel sounds. (The vowel system is so complex that I can't give a precise number, as we'll see shortly.) Before you get scared off completely, I should mention that as a speaker of English, you already know all these vowels because you use them in speaking and listening every day, and you also know a huge amount about how to read and spell them. What we're doing here is bringing this knowledge into more conscious awareness so that we can apply it to understanding better what children are doing in learning to read and write.

The most important quality that defines the nature of a particular vowel is where it occurs in the mouth. This is a little less obvious for vowels than for consonants; for a /b/ the lips are definitely together, but what exactly is going on in the mouth when we produce the vowel sound in *bat*? Although the position of the tongue changes from one vowel to another, it's hard to define precisely because it varies from person to person—and from word to word for any one person. But it's possible to design a paradigm that shows roughly where the vowels occur in the mouth, particularly in relation to each other. The two tables below show thirteen simple vowel sounds and three *diphthongs*, which glide from one location to another. (The latter are often called glides, but I'll refer to them only as diphthongs, to avoid confusion with the consonant glides. Some of the vowels in the first table [e.g., /ā/ and /ō/] are often glided, and many Southern speakers make diphthongs of vowels that other speakers don't, but the three vowels in the second table are always glided.)

Thirteen English Vowels

	FRONT	CENTRAL	BACK
HIGH	beat /ē/		boot /u/
	bit /ɪ/		book /ʊ/
MID	bait /ā/	about /ə/, father /ɚ/	boat /ō/
	bet /ɛ/		bought /ɔ/
LOW	bat /æ/	but /ʌ/	hot /o/

Three English Diphthongs

	FRONT	CENTRAL	BACK
HIGH	/ɪ/		/ʊ/
MID			/ɔ/ boy /ɔi/
LOW		/a/ how /au/ high /aɪ/	

Categorizing vowels by position in the mouth is unfamiliar to many educators, so I'd like to point out how these categories differ from categories you may already know. Teachers often refer to long and short vowels (five of each), and nine of these occur in the tables above. First, find the vowels we usually refer to as long *a*, *e*, *i*, and *o*. (We also refer to these as the letters saying their own names.) Three of them are in the first table, in *bait*, *beat*, and *boat*, while long *i* is a diphthong (*high*). Where's long *u*? The sound that we typically refer to by this name, which is the one we hear at the beginning of *useful*, is actually a consonant-plus-vowel combination, /yu/. (The spelling of words like *Yukon* reflects this.)

Next, find the short vowels, the ones that often occur when we have a single vowel letter in the middle of a three-letter word. These all occur in the first table, in *bat*, *bet*, *bit*, *hot*, and *but*.

Even though we've covered the long and the short vowels, there are still several other sounds in the tables. We can perhaps grasp them most easily by thinking of them as falling into two groups. First, there are a number of vowels (other than some of the long and short ones) in which the lips are rounded. Three of these are high back and mid back vowels, as heard in *boot*, *book*, and *bought*. The other two are diphthongs; the vowel in *how* (/au/) ends up rounded and in the same position as the vowel in *book*, while the vowel in *boy* (/ɔi/) starts out rounded and in the same position as the vowel in *bought*.

To further complicate things, these rounded vowels vary geographically. Many Americans, particularly west of the Mississippi, as well as most Canadians, don't distinguish between the vowels of *hot* and *bought*, at least in most words. A simple test for this is whether you pronounce the names *Don* and *Dawn* the same or differently. If they're the same for you, you have one phoneme (probably closer to /o/ than to /ɔ/) where other North American English speakers have two. (This is why the number of vowel phonemes in English varies from speaker to speaker.) Another geographic variation: a distinctive feature of many Canadians' speech is a pronunciation of the vowel in words like *out* that's close to the vowel in *boot*.

The two remaining vowels are mid-central ones that occur in unaccented syllables. One of them is our friend the schwa, while the other is the related sound that occurs in the second syllable of *father*. This sound is often described as the schwa plus an /r/, but in practice it's usually phonetically a single sound (i.e., the position of the mouth doesn't change in making it) and I think this is the most useful way to describe it. I also love the name of this sound; it's called a *schwar*! Its symbol (/ɚ/) looks like a schwa with a little tail added on for the *r* part.

You may wonder why I haven't talked about r-controlled vowels (other than /ɚ/), since they are discussed in so many basal reader programs. First, it's very hard to get a feel for which vowels actually occur before the /r/ in words like *fair* and *four*. Second, to give examples of all the different vowel sounds followed by /r/ would be extremely tedious. Third, there's a lot of variation in how r-controlled vowels are pronounced. For instance, for some speakers *cores* and *Coors* are homophones while for others they're not, and sometimes words like *fire* come out as two syllables (/fī-ɚ/). For the nonspecialist, it's easiest just to say that vowel sounds are somewhat distorted when followed by an /r/, and that they're likely to be harder to spell than other vowels.

What's the Difference Between Diphthongs, Digraphs, and Blends?

A *diphthong*, as we've seen, is a vowel phoneme that glides from one spot in the mouth to another. The word comes from Greek roots meaning *two* (*di-*) and *voice* or *sound* (*phthongos*), so you can think of diphthongs as phonemes that contain two sounds. *Blend* also refers to sounds: specifically, two or more consonant sounds occurring in sequence but retaining their own identity, like the first two sounds in *blond* or the first three in *string*. A *digraph*, by contrast, refers to the spelling of a sound; two (*di-*) letters (*graph*) that represent a single sound like *ng* or *sh*. These terms can be confusing, because a word occasionally contains examples of all three. For instance, *thrice* begins with a blend of which one phoneme (/θ/) is spelled with a digraph, and its vowel is a diphthong. This table may help you keep the three terms straight:

	refers to	type of sound	sounds	phonemes	letters	examples
diphthong	sound	vowel	2	1	1 or 2	boy, cider
blend	sound	consonant	2 or 3	2 or 3	2 or 3	flip, string
digraph	spelling	vowel or consonant	1	1	2	thing, keep

Why Does the Same Sound Not Always Sound the Same?

As literate adults who are familiar not only with the sounds of words but with their spellings, it's easy for us to think that the pronunciation of English sounds is more regular than it is. But not only is there variation from one speaker to another, we also all pronounce the same phoneme in slightly different ways depending on the word. Here are some examples (described in nontechnical ways):

/n/ in *when* and *went* (the second one is less prominent)
/t/ in *late* and *later* (the second one is like a /d/)
/p/ in *spin* and *pin* (the second one has a slight puff of air after it)
/l/ in *like* and *pill* (the first sounds "light," the second, "dark")

   You probably weren't aware of most if any of these differences, because they're subphonemic, which means they don't distinguish one phoneme from another. (The different versions of each phoneme are known as allophones [meaning "other sound"], which are predictable phonetic variations.) They occur for reasons having to do mostly with ease of articulation; for instance, in *went* it's natural to not pronounce the /n/ very strongly in the transition from the vowel to the /t/. Similar differences distinguish phonemes in other languages; for instance, aspiration—the puff of air in *pin*—is phonemic in Thai, so that an English speaker learning Thai would have to learn to make a distinction between /tam/ (to pound) and /tʰam/ (to do), but would be inclined to pronounce both of them like the latter since /t/'s before vowels are aspirated in English (Fromkin & Rodman 1993, p. 227).

   These small differences in pronunciation fortunately don't really concern us in reading and writing, since our spelling system doesn't represent this level of detail. However, children don't always realize this, and we might see evidence that they don't in their comments and invented spellings. Two examples: children often omit *m* and *n* before other consonants, not because they can't hear them but because they recognize that what they're hearing isn't quite the same as a regular /m/, /n/, or /ŋ/ (Read 1971, 1975). Phonetically, these are the differences between *when*, *went*, and *wet*:

	when	**went**	**wet**
vowel nasalized?	yes	yes	no
/n/ pronounced?	yes	often not	N/A
phonemic representation	/wɛn/ (or /hwɛn/)	/wɛnt/	/wɛt/
phonetic representation	[wɛ̃n]	[wɛ̃t] (often)	[wɛt]

(A tilde (~) over a vowel means that it's nasalized, so that air goes out the nose as well as the mouth.)

   An invented spelling like WET for *went* is therefore more like a detailed phonetic transcription than it is like the standard spelling, which represents the underlying phonemes rather than the way they come out phonetically. I once saw a second grader spell *went* correctly, then go back and erase the *n*. He explained, "It's sort of like there's an *n* there, but not really." I don't think a linguist could explain it much better!

The spelling BLATER that a first grader wrote for *bladder* also makes sense when we think about phonetic variation. When either a /t/ or a /d/ appears between two vowel sounds, it typically turns into a quick tongue flap against the roof of the mouth that sounds more like /d/ than /t/. (The precise phonetic symbol for it is [D].) Children therefore often understandably use *d* in spelling words like *later* and *water*. But in the BLATER example, the child appears to have enough knowledge of English to realize that such words are spelled with *t* even though that's not quite what you hear; in this case she just overgeneralized to a word that should have had a *d* in the first place. The reason for the *t* in *later* is transparent to us since we can hear it in *late*, but why is *bladder* spelled with a *d* and *water* with a *t*? The spellings relate back to the individual words' histories, which our spelling preserves even though our pronunciation doesn't distinguish them.

TWO

Phonics Rules

Here's what you've been waiting for—the simple rules you can teach kids so that they can sound out any word they come to. Sorry! That's not the way it is, regardless of what many educators and members of the general public think. This doesn't mean there aren't phonics rules, but they're complex and limited in their application. By phonics rules, I mean letter-sound relationships that we can use for reading. These overlap with the spelling rules that we use for writing, but not completely.

To be more specific about what we mean by phonics rules: they enable us to look at a *grapheme* (one or more letters working as a unit) and know what sound is likely to be associated with it. (One of the tricky parts is knowing when two letters are a digraph or represent two separate sounds, like the *gh* in *coughing* and *bighorn*, respectively.) They also enable us to read nonsense words such as *floop*. However, K. Goodman (1993) explores at length how we can't assume that letters "represent" sounds in any simple way, if at all. As a context for my discussion here, it's important to realize that readers primarily deal with text as a whole and that shifting their focus to letters and sounds is useful mainly when stuck, because it risks derailing the process of reading for meaning. Much of our processing of phonics goes on below the level of conscious awareness.

In this chapter, I'm not going to talk about how this knowledge works in the reading process or the details of how children acquire it; my goal is to help you, as an educator, become familiar with phonics rules. So I'm going to lay out the most important rules, and I'll also share some thoughts about which ones kids are likely to pick up on their own given the right kinds of experiences, which ones are too complicated or inconsistent to be worth learning formally, and which ones are likely to be amenable to some teaching. To echo Goldilocks: we can classify phonics rules as too easy, too hard (or too unimportant), and just right.

Which Rules Are Too Easy?

Once children have learned the names of the alphabet letters (see McGee & Richgels 1989 for some ways to support this process holistically), they have the knowledge they need to associate many letters with the sounds they represent, particularly consonant sounds. For instance, a child who knows that /bē/ is the name of the symbol *b* is equipped to know what sound *bird* starts with when she sees it in print.

The following table shows fourteen consonant letters (Column A), the phonetic spellings of their names (Column B), and the phonemes they typically represent (Column C); in all cases, the names of these letters connect with the sounds they usually represent. Charles Read (1975), in his work with preschool writers who were using invented spelling, found that they represented the regular consonant sounds very consistently. The percentages in Column D show just how consistently—how often the children Read worked with spelled the phonemes in Column C with the letter in Column A, figures that reflect what teachers typically see in young children's invented spelling. Treiman (1993), looking at the invented spellings of first graders, found comparable but somewhat lower percentages; her figures are in Column E. The only ones that are below 73% for Read or 65% for Treiman are /j/, /k/ (spelled with *k* or *q*), and /z/, each of which has another frequent spelling (*g*, *c*, and *s* respectively).

A	B	C	D	E
b	/bē/	/b/	94.5%	89.2%
d	/dē/	/d/	73.3%	65.3%
f	/ɛf/	/f/	92.5%	91.8%
j	/ʃā/	/ʃ/	35.6%	n/a
k	/kā/	/k/	40.3%	41.4%
l	/ɛl/	/l/	82.0%	70.7%
m	/em/	/m/	88.5%	84.8%
n	/ɛn/	/n/	85.2%	71.2%
p	/pē/	/p/	93.2%	83.7%
q	/kyu/	/k/	0.9%	1.6%
r	/or/	/r/	89.0%	79.6%
s	/ɛs/	/s/	87.0%	84.4%
t	/tē/	/t/	83.2%	74.9%
v	/vē/	/v/	91.3%	75.8%
z	/zē/	/z/	3.7%	9.9%

Projecting from Read's and Treiman's work, if children have internalized the rule, To spell [sound in Column C], use [corresponding letter in Column A], I think it's reasonable to suggest that a child who can figure out that /dɔg/ starts with the letter *d* can also realize that a printed word starting with d has /d/ as its first sound (once she's grasped the principle that letters can map on to sounds). Or, put formally, When you see [letter from Column A], whose name is pronounced [as in Column B], it's likely to represent [corresponding sound from Column C]. For reading (though not for spelling), the letters *j, k, q,* and *z* are consistent and would fit this pattern. A discussion of how children get to this point comes in Chapter 3; my message now is that these phonics rules all follow the same principle—the name of the letter contains the sound of the letter. If children are showing in their invented spelling that they've made this connection, they certainly won't need minilessons on each of these letter-sound correspondences. (Why teach them what they already know?)

Which Rules Are Just Right?

There are a number of phonics relationships that aren't obvious from the names of the letters but that are consistent enough that it may make some sense to help children learn about them. However, it's crucial to realize that any instruction of this kind should accompany and follow experiences with reading, not precede them. Moustafa (1993, 1995) has made a very strong case that children can unconsciously abstract knowledge about phonics from experiences with predictable text. Any instruction should serve primarily as a brief supplement to this core experience. And all of my suggestions for minilessons are only relevant for kids who aren't yet applying the principles involved, which in most cases means the early primary grades. A child who can read a nonsense word like *hig* doesn't need instruction in reading *h*.

I've based the rules here and in the "too hard" section on Clymer (1963), who assesses the usefulness of forty-five commonly taught phonics rules. The patterns that seem of some value for instruction fall into three groups: single-letter vowel spellings, two-letter vowel spellings, and some consonants.

Single-Letter Vowels

The letters *a*, *e*, *i*, *o*, and *u* often take on a "short" pronunciation, most often when one of these is the only vowel letter in a one-syllable word, like *cat*, and is not followed by *r*. When one of them occurs in a longer word, things get trickier; the first vowel in *happy* is short but in *lady* is long. We can say that a vowel sound is usually short before a double consonant in a longer word, but what about words like *esophagus* and *escalator*? *Esophagus* (/ɪ-so-fə-gəs/) has two short vowels and two schwas, escalator (/ɛs-kə-lā-tɚ/) has one short, one long, one schwa, and one schwar. Clearly, whatever helps us read the vowels in words like these can't be a consciously applied set of rules but must be a more general, implicit knowledge of letter-sound relationships. (Adams [1990] points out that knowing where the vowels are in a word is almost as useful as knowing which vowels they are; without vowels, although it's not quickly obvious that *prcpn* is *porcupine*, it's very easy to tell what *d*ff*d*l* is.) And before *r*, even in single-syllable words, all bets are off; *a* sounds like /o/ (*car*, *bar*, etc.), *o* may sound like /ō/

26

(*for, nor*), and *e*, *i*, and *u* sound the same (*her, sir,* and *cur*). Therefore, formal learning about the sounds of single-letter vowels seems useful only for short words without an *r* after the vowel; teachers often explore these patterns through word families (*cat, bat, rat; hit, bit, sit*), which don't need to be covered at great length but can be used to establish the idea that if you know *cat* you can also read *bat* and *rat*.

Two-Letter Vowels

The most commonly known version of a rule for two-letter vowel spellings is, When two vowels go walking, the first one does the talking (i.e., "says its name"). Clymer found, in a database of 2,600 primary-grade words, that this was true only 45% of the time (309 words like *bead*, where it worked, 377 like *chief*, where it didn't). However, an expanded version of the rule, although it doesn't work all that often, could be used in a commonsense way to help children think about what to do when they come across more than one vowel in a short, single-syllable word (although whether a word has one or two syllables isn't always obvious, as we can see in *crease* and *create*).

Here's the way I'd phrase it (not as a rule but as a comment): When you see a short word that has two vowels together, or a vowel followed by a *w* or *y*, or an *e* at the end, trying the long sound of the first vowel is a good first guess (except for double *o*). (In practice, I'd use a series of several minilessons to explore this idea.) Here are examples of those four cases:

Pattern	Example where it works	Example where it doesn't	How often it works (according to Clymer)
two vowels together	leaf	head	45% of the time
vowel followed by *w*	crow	threw	40%
vowel followed by *y*	tray	buy	Clymer didn't determine (but 78% for *ay*)
e at the end	bone	done	63%

Why even bother to try this rule if it works so seldom? Because it's general enough to apply to a lot of words, and is better than nothing. But it has to be used in conjunction with thinking, Does this come out as a word at all, and as a word that makes sense within the context?

Readers also need to know what to do if this rule doesn't work, because there's no second rule to go to. The only thing that makes sense if the rule doesn't work, which is what we'd do as adults if we read a nonsense word and were told we were wrong (e.g., if we pronounced *pove* to rhyme with *rove*), is to try another pronunciation, which we typically do without thinking of a rule, perhaps by using an analogy to another word (e.g., could *pove* rhyme with *love*?).

Double *o* is a special case; it can represent either /u/, as in *food* (most of the time), or /ʊ/, as in *foot* (in about fifteen common words [Venezky 1970]). We have to try both and see which one produces a word we recognize.

That's it for stuff that's worth teaching about vowels.

Consonants

There are three sets of generalizations about consonants that aren't as obvious as those in the "too easy" section above but that are useful enough to be worth exploring with children. First of all, there are three simple letter-sound relationships that don't happen to coincide with the names of the letters involved: the letters at the beginning of *hat*, *wig*, and *yet*. These letters represent their respective sounds pretty consistently at the beginning of a word or syllable, but not elsewhere, as we see in *oh*, *blow*, and *day*. A minilesson might involve listing and reading words, some familiar and some not, that start with (for instance) *w* or *y* and asking children to talk about what they notice and thus form their own generalizations. Second, the digraphs that appear at the beginning of *chin*, *shin*, and *phone* represent the sounds heard at the beginning of those words pretty consistently, and the *th* digraph represents either of two sounds, which are pretty predictable from context. (That is, if *thing* and *thank* were pronounced with the /ð/ of *the* and *this* rather than /θ/, or vice versa, the result wouldn't be real words. *Thy/thigh* is one of the few exceptions.) Third, the letters *c* and *g* usually represent /s/ and /j/ before *e*, *i*, and *y*, and are always pronounced /k/ and /g/ before other letters, as seen in the following table:

	"Soft" sound before *e*, *i*, or *y*	"Hard" sound before *e*, *i*, or *y*	"Hard" sound before other letters
c	city (96% of the time)	no examples	cat
g	gene (64% of the time)	give	green
Percentages come from Clymer.			

Which Rules Are Too Hard or Too Useless?

Given how few phonics rules are clear and useful enough to be worth teaching, what in the world has been filling up all those basal readers all these years? Let's take a look.

In his 1963 study, Clymer used 2,600 words likely to be encountered in the primary grades to explore the accuracy of forty-five phonics generalizations appearing in basal readers. I'm not going to take the space to run through many of these incredibly boring rules, but would like to point out how minimally useful many of them are likely to be. (And since sound-letter relationships in English haven't changed in any big ways since 1963, a similar listing of rules from today's basal readers wouldn't be much different.) Here are some representative ones, arranged in order of decreasing usefulness:

Generalization	Example	Counter-example	Usefulness
1. When a word begins with *kn*, the *k* is silent.	knife	—	100% of 10 words
2. When the letter *i* is followed by the letters *gh*, the *i* usually stands for its long sound and the *gh* is silent.	high	neighbor	71% of 31 words

3. When *e* is followed by *w*, the vowel sound is the same as represented by *oo*.	blew	sew	35% of 27 words
4. When *a* follows *w* in a word, it usually has the sound [it does in *water*].	watch	swam	32% of 47 words
5. When *y* is used as a vowel in words, it sometimes has the sound of long *i*.	fly	funny	15% of 199 words

Clearly the usefulness of such rules is pretty limited; if they're accurate, they're likely not to apply to many words, and if they apply to a larger number of words, they're often wrong more than they're right! I challenge you to come up with *any* other phonics rules worth teaching beyond the ones I've described in the "just right" section above, rules that could be justified by their applying (a) to a reasonably large number of words and (b) with a reasonable level of accuracy.

Given the small number of phonics rules that are worth teaching, how do basal readers claim to provide so much instruction in phonics? Primarily by teaching patterns that I've described as being too easy or too hard to be worth teaching! I think there can be a place, for instance, for acquainting children with the silent *k* in words like *knife* as part of a quick, informal minilesson, but not for teaching it formally with a series of lessons, worksheets, reviews, and tests. These minor patterns don't deserve a lot of time and energy but are probably best picked up through brief discussion as kids notice and comment on them.

What conclusion, then, should we draw from this overview of phonics rules? Perhaps that once we get much beyond simple observations of letter-sound relationships, like *b* representing /b/ and two contiguous vowel letters representing a "long" sound, phonics rules get far too complex and picky to be worth studying formally.

What About Syllabication? (Or Is It Syllabification?)
Does It Help Kids Read Better?

The word *syllabification* always transports me back to Mr. Paul's eighth-grade LA-SS (language arts/social studies) class, where, if memory serves, we had exercises every week on dividing words into syllables and a special place on the bulletin board where our syllabification papers were posted. (By the way, *syllabification* and *syllabication* are synonyms. I think Mr. Paul just chose whenever possible to use the bigger of two words!) Despite my having been indoctrinated at a young age into the importance of syllables, I think it's a virtually useless topic. Theoretically, it's true that vowels in open syllables (e.g., those ending with a vowel) tend to be long and those in closed syllables (those ending with a consonant) short. But there's no predictable way of knowing if a syllable is open or closed just from looking at a word. For instance, *cat-e-chism* starts with a closed syllable and *ca-ter-ing* with an open one, but their first four letters are the same. Clymer found that the "rule" that the first syllable in a word is open if its vowel is followed by a single consonant was true only 44% of the time (i.e., you'd do better by guessing).

The other reason we all used to learn a lot about syllables related to the esthetics of typing. When writing by hand, you can even out the margins without breaking words into syllables, but when I worked as a secretary in the 1960s, I used the hyphen key on the typewriter a lot to divide words at the end of a line. These days, with computers able to justify text right and left (literally), the only people who need to be meticulous about how words are hyphenated are copy editors of typeset books. (Mr. Paul is probably retired by now, but I sometimes wonder if he could still be out there doing those bulletin boards . . .)

THREE

Spelling Rules

Although we use much of the same body of knowledge for spelling as we do for the graphophonic part of reading, it's not quite reciprocal, because we're coming at it from a different direction. When we read, we're establishing what sound goes with a particular letter; when we spell, we're establishing what letter or letters we need to represent a particular sound. The other big difference between reading and spelling has to do with focus and attention, particularly at early developmental levels. Young readers usually retell a text globally, recognize whole words, or both, whereas young writers spontaneously attempt to find a way to represent sound-letter relationships as they attend to each phoneme (Bissex 1980).

We can think of the sound-letter relationships we use for spelling as falling into three groups: consistent defaults (which work for most of the consonants and a few vowels), variants (which apply to most of the vowels and a few consonants), and orthographic patterns, which work on a level higher than the single phoneme. Also, it's important to realize that the sound-letter relationships of spelling occur within a larger context where the spelling of words represents their meanings and origins as well as their sounds, and that spelling is consistent even when speakers aren't. For instance, the *d* in *educate* reflects its relationship to *educe* and occurs not only in the spelling of Britons, who say *ed-yoo-cate* but in that of Americans, who say *edge-a-cate*. (See K. Goodman 1993 for a fuller discussion.)

Which Sounds Have a Default Spelling?

I'm using the term *default spelling* to refer to the way a sound is usually spelled when there's no reason for it to be spelled differently. That's not as cryptic as it sounds. Here's an example: /p/ is usually spelled *p*, but sometimes it needs to be doubled, as in *copper* (to make the *o* short) or *tipped* (to keep the *i* short after adding the suffix). Similarly, /f/ is usually spelled *f* but typically doubles at the ends of words following a single vowel (e.g., *stiff*).

Most of the consonants have a default spelling represented by the same single letter that we use in the phonetic symbol; these are the stops /b/, /d/, /g/, /p/, and /t/; the fricatives /f/, /v/, /s/, and /z/; the nasals /m/ and /n/; and the liquids and glides /l/, /r/, /h/, /w/, and /y/. The five short vowels also have a single-letter default spelling, as seen in the words *bat*, *bet*, *bit*, *hot*, and *but*.

Five consonants have a two-letter default spelling; /ŋ/ is *ng*, both /θ/ and /ð/ are *th*, /š/ is *sh*, and /č/ is *ch*. The four remaining consonants are less consistent but three of them are still predictable; /ž/ doesn't have one consistent spelling, but /k/, /ʝ/, and /s/ are affected by the letters that follow them. Before *e*, *i*, and *y*, /k/ has to be spelled *k* (as in *kill*), while elsewhere *c* is usual but not obligatory (*cat* but also *kale*). For /ʝ/ and /s/, only *j* and *s*, respectively, can occur before letters other than *e*, *i*, and *y*, while *g* and *c* can appear before those three letters. Confused? Here's a table laying it out (the more common spelling in each instance is listed first):

Before	a	e	i	l	o	r	u	y
/k/	cat	—	—	clam	coat	crab	cup	—
	kale	keep	kill	klutz	koala	krait	kudzu	Kyle
/ʝ/	jag	jet	jig	n/a	jog	n/a	jug	—
	—	gem	gin	—	—		—	gym
/s/	sag	set	sit	slip	sob	n/a	sup	syrup
	—	cell	cite	—	—		—	cycle

What should children learn about these patterns? If they are not only aware of the variant ways to spell these sounds but are also good enough readers to know that *cill* can't spell *kill* and *gump* can't spell *jump*, a minilesson can help them make their knowledge more explicit. A class or small group could construct a version of the table above with the teacher's guidance as a tool for discovering for themselves how these spellings are patterned.

Which Sounds Have Variant Spellings?

All of the consonants and five of the vowels have a default, or predictable, spelling, but the remaining vowels can be spelled in a number of ways, with no one spelling occurring almost all of the time, although position in the word has an effect. The following table gives examples for each of these vowels (these are only examples; position in the word affects but usually doesn't determine which spelling will occur):

Phoneme	Single-syllable word	Longer word	End of word or syllable
/ā/	rain, gate	major	tray
/ē/	leaf, team, gene	ether	free, be
/ī/	bite, light	minus	by
/ō/	coat, bone	bonus	throw
/ɔ/	talk, taut, fog	water	law
/u/	food, brute	tuna, balloon	true, igloo
/ʊ/	book, push	bushel	n/a
/au/	loud, bout	counter	cow
/ɔi/	boil	poison, oyster	boy
/ə/	unpredictable; depends on word (about, clueless, crisis, propel, circus, anxious, etc.)		
/ɚ/ (unstressed)	n/a	vermouth, surprise	father

As with reading, the less that spelling patterns are predictable, the less useful it is to try to teach children about them, since we can't provide any definitive rules that work all the time. I've written more extensively about these vowel patterns and how to teach them in *You Kan Red This!* (1992), but it comes down to helping children realize that knowledge about how to spell these vowel sounds can usually help us come up with at least a good invented spelling for an unknown word, but that we'll need to check and make sure of the correct spelling until we've learned the word. The table is a teacher reference and can help in planning minilessons. For instance, to explore /ā/, you could ask children to come up with words containing the sound and group them by spelling pattern. Those in the table are most common, but others are found in *weigh, hey, rein,* and so on. You can then help children make generalizations about how to spell /ā/ in an unknown word: for instance, make a reasonable guess based on the patterns, then check.

Which Spellings Are Influenced by Orthographic Patterns?

If we look beyond how individual phonemes are spelled, we can find a little more information about English spelling in the form of patterns that apply to the spelling of many sounds across a particular word environment. The three most important are final silent *e* (which is also a part of the variant vowels described above), double consonants, and changes in words before suffixes (changing *y* to *i*, dropping final silent *e*, and consonant doubling).

When we see *e* at the end of a word, it's usually silent and often means that the preceding vowel is long, particularly in one-syllable words. Although there are plenty of exceptions (*have, love, -le* words like *cable, -dge* words like *badge*), and although long-vowel words are spelled in ways other than with final *e*, this pattern is useful enough to be a valuable tool for both reading and spelling. The final *e* drops off before suffixes starting with a vowel because we no longer need it to show that the vowel is long. Double consonants serve the opposite purpose, showing that a vowel is short. This occurs within words (*hammer*) and before suffixes (*hopping*). Again, this is a useful pattern, even though English has other double consonants that are less easy to explain (*brass, giraffe*). The change of *y* to *i* occurs because *y* usually doesn't represent a vowel when it's not at the end of a word (Cummings 1988), which is why *sillyest* looks funny, as if it rhymed with *pill fest*. Here's an overview of the rules for changes before suffixes:

WHAT'S A SCHWA SOUND ANYWAY?

Root word pattern	Before *s*	Before *ing*	Before *er, ed*
consonant + *y* (hurry)	*y* changes to *ie** (hurries)	no change (hurrying)	*y* changes to *i* (hurried)
one vowel, one consonant (pin)	no change (pins)	consonant doubles (pinning)	consonant doubles (pinned)
silent final *e* (pine)	no change (pines)	*e* drops out (pining)	*e* drops out (pined)

*More technically, *y* changes to *i* and an *e* is added to preserve the vowel pronunciation; otherwise, we'd have *hurris*, which would read like *Harris*.

Why Does Our Spelling System Seem So Illogical?

There's a three-word answer: geography, history, semantics.

First, English has incorporated words from many different languages, not only its Germanic roots and the extensive body of words with Romance language origins but globally. Words that would probably be spelled *cacky*, *lazonya*, and *noo* if our spelling system were phonetically logical are instead *khaki*, *lasagna*, and *gnu*, which seem a little strange to our eyes because they've retained much of how they were spelled in Hindi, Italian, and Khoikhoi (an African language), respectively. What we lack in alphabetic logic we make up for in diversity; personally I find these spellings more appealing than the phonetic ones, since they retain the flavor of their original language (just as I was gratified to see that a Native American nation in Nova Scotia now refers to itself as the Mi'kmaqs rather than the anglicized term Micmacs prevalent twenty years ago).

As for history, spoken language changes more rapidly than spelling, so that our spelling system preserves older pronunciations. For instance, the *k* in words like *knife* used to be pronounced, as were the silent final *e*'s in many words. My prediction is that in fifty years or so, the difference between *wh* and *w* will be pretty well gone from most American speech just like the pronunciation of *k* in *knife*, but of course *which*, *when*, and *whale* won't become *wich*, *wen*, and *wale*.

36

The semantic nature of spelling has to do with related words' having similar spellings despite predictable variation or historical change in pronunciation. Thus *nation* is spelled like *native*, not "nashun," and *one*, which used to be pronounced like the first syllable of the related word *only*, is still spelled analogously even though it's now pronounced "wun" (which is, of course, a common invented spelling for it). Actually, our spelling system only seems illogical if we expect it should be purely alphabetic rather than reflect the multifaceted, complex nature of language.

Where Do Spelling Rules Fit into the Bigger Picture of Learning How to Spell?

As we've seen, spelling rules aren't any more comprehensive than phonics rules. (I've written elsewhere [1990] about how and why spelling textbooks spend so much time on rules.) This doesn't mean that sound-letter relationships are completely useless in learning how to spell, since we do after all have an alphabetic language. As an adult spelling a word you've never seen before, you'd be able to come up with a pretty good invention, based largely on what you know about sound-letter relationships. (By contrast, I presume that a literate Chinese adult could only make a wild guess at the character for a word she'd never seen before.) However, spelling isn't ultimately about coming up with pretty good inventions, it's about coming up with the (usually) single conventionally accepted spelling for each word. Therefore a lot of formal teaching of rules and patterns that aren't very definitive doesn't seem a good use of time, but we *can* spend some productive time helping children think about those patterns (which their invented spellings show they're thinking about already) and bring them a little more into conscious awareness. If a child can say, "I don't know how to spell *leaf*, but LEEF and LEAF are my best guesses because I see those patterns in a lot of words," she has a good sense of how spelling patterns work in English. If she goes on to say, "I'll use these two guesses to check in the dictionary when I'm editing my story," all the better.

FOUR

The Speakers of English: Issues of Language Variation

You say potato, I say potahto. People in the United States stick to *skedge-els* while the British have *shed-yools*. Bostonians *pahk* the *cah*, while Southerners have *cay-uts* and *dawgs* for pets. Anybody with a television, anyone who's traveled, knows that speakers of English talk differently from one other. Yet we all read and write a highly uniform version of English whose spelling in particular doesn't change according to the author's pronunciation.

Since one aspect of written language consists of relationships between sounds and letters, it's natural to wonder whether learning to read and spell will be affected by the different ways people talk. For instance, will the child who pronounces *pen* and *pin* the same have trouble reading and spelling them correctly?

This question should have a simple, empirical answer, but there's a great deal of misunderstanding about language variation—why it occurs, what it means, what effects it has—that's complicated by all the political issues to which it is inextricably connected. So although this chapter's ultimate goal is to answer the question, If people talk differently, will it affect their reading and spelling? we need first to understand what we mean when we say "people talk differently."

Why Do Speakers of English Sound So Different From One Another?

As with many aspects of language, it's a matter of history and geography. As groups of people migrated over time and became cut off from their old communities, their language changed. It's the nature of all language to change over time, and when groups become geographically separated, their languages start to diverge. If the change is great enough that the speakers of two groups no longer understand one another, we say that they speak two different languages (such as French and Spanish, which are related but distinct). (This is a slight oversimplification, since sometimes two closely related languages are somewhat mutually intelligible [Fromkin & Rodman 1993], but it's accurate enough for our purposes.) When we hear a speaker of English who sounds very different from us, the reason we know it's still English is that we can eventually understand him after our ear gets used to his speech.

Within the United States, these variations aren't great, but we may find some British speakers hard to understand. For instance, several years ago when I saw a movie, *Letter to Brezhnev*, that was set in working-class Liverpool, I found myself wishing for subtitles during the first part of the movie. But as I settled into the story, I also settled into the characters' speech and had no further trouble understanding it (and indeed found some of the differences interesting, such as the characters' pronouncing the f-word—which was used frequently!—to rhyme with book). I had a similar experience with the 1996 movie *Trainspotting*, set in Scotland.

With the rise of mass media, speakers of different versions of English are exposed to one another's language more than they used to be, but it remains to be seen what effects this will have on the nature and pace of language change. At any rate, however, language differences grow out of language communities. There are also linguistic constraints on language change: because of the nature of language and the way that humans process it, languages and versions of a single language diverge from one another not randomly but in predictable ways, such as simplification, regularization, and the elimination of re-dundancy (Wolfram 1991).

Versions of a language differ across multiple dimensions: pragmatics (such as different ways of showing politeness), vocabulary (what's called a *sofa* in the United States is a *chesterfield* in Canada), grammar (*shall* is used more in England than in the United States), and pronunciation. However, for the purposes of this discussion I focus almost entirely on pronunciational (phonological) differences, since they're the ones that are relevant when thinking about phonics and spelling.

Are Language Differences Just Geographic?

Let's look at all the different kinds of language communities in English. First, there's the national dimension: the United States, Canada, Great Britain, Australia, and a number of other countries have large numbers of native speakers of English, with versions that are more British (as in Australia) and versions that are more American (as in Canada). Since North America has been home to English speakers for only a few centuries and its speakers are already very different from the British, it's clear that the pace of change within a language can be quite rapid.

Second, within a country there are regional variations. In the United States, among the most distinct regional versions of English are New England and Southern speech, both with subgroups. For instance, although I was raised in New Jersey and can't personally distinguish different Southern accents, native Southerners have told me that not only can they tell what state someone is from but often what town and sometimes even what neighborhood. Mapping the dialects of the United States is a complex exercise that has been written about extensively (see Wolfram 1991 for a readable introduction). Since the bulk of language learning takes place in childhood, the version of English we speak is basically the one we were exposed to as children, although we may change it somewhat or add variations as we grow older.

What's a Dialect, What's an Accent, and Who Has Them?

The term *accent* is typically used in a nontechnical way to describe speech whose pronunciation stands out as "different," usually meaning different from that of the speaker, and is used to describe both speakers of English as a second language (a French accent) and native speakers from a region other than one's own (a Maine accent).

The term *dialect* is often used in everyday speech to refer to a distinctive form of a language (e.g., the Cockney dialect), but in linguistics it refers to *any* version of a language, so that we can refer to upper-class Boston speech, working-class Minnesota speech, and California surfer talk as a few of the many dialects of American English. We all speak a dialect, by definition. However, it's also important to know that a dialect is an abstraction, a description of a set of features, rather than a definition of how any one person talks; any individual's speech is subject to multiple influences.

Language also varies across groups within a community, the most important being ethnic and social-class. Ethnic differences in language are not, of course, genetic, but reflect the language communities out of which they grow. The more that groups are socially separated within a community, the more likely those groups are to speak differently, which is why, for instance, working-class and upper-middle-class speakers within the same city will sound more dissimilar than people from the same social class that live many miles apart.

Two examples. When I lived in New Brunswick, Canada, I was aware of groups of people who lived only a mile or two apart yet whose speech was noticeably different from each other even though their social class was comparable. The first was a Micmac reservation and the adjoining English Canadian town, the second was the border town of St. Stephen and the adjoining United States town (separated only by a narrow river) of Calais, Maine. In both cases, although there was a fair amount of daily intermingling (the Micmacs shopped and often worked in town, and the people of St. Stephen regularly shopped across the border and even shared a fire department with

Calais), the communities in which children grew up and learned to speak were separate, so that you could clearly identify which community someone was from the minute that she opened her mouth.

Ethnic variation in language (as in the case of the Micmacs) accompanies communities, whether local or national, defined by ethnicity. Some of the features found in the speech of African Americans are a heritage from African languages while others are similar to the speech of white Southerners (since most American blacks can trace their ancestry back to the Confederate states as well as to Africa), and these features persist (with more recent additions) because African Americans constitute a distinct community and culture in American society. In fact, the New York Times recently suggested that differences between Black English and other forms of American speech appear to be increasing, apparently due to the increased social alienation of inner-city communities. Linguist William Labov commented, "It's the present, not the past, that's creating this division" (Holmes 1996).

Most white Americans are part of a homogenized culture linguistically; I'm of half-Swedish, half-German ancestry, but this hasn't left me speaking any differently from my friends with Irish or Armenian forebears. Latino Americans often, however, speak an English that's still influenced by Spanish, while many Native Americans also have subtle distinctive language features when they speak English (see Leap 1993). Both of these examples reflect second-language influence, since the other language is still an active presence in the communities involved.

Even the speech of speakers whose first language is English may reflect features of a second language. When I taught on an Ojibway reservation, I was taken aback at first to hear children occasionally use male and female pronouns interchangeably; for instance, a first grader watching a female teammate step up to bat at softball said, "Wow! He's going to hit the ball really far!" When I learned a little about Ojibway and discovered that it has a single genderless pronoun that means *he, she, it,* or *they* depending on the context, I understood what was going on. The adults in the community who had learned English as a second language weren't used to distinguishing pronouns by gender and therefore didn't use them consistently in English. (The equivalent is an English speaker learning Spanish, who has to learn two different words for the, *el* and *la*, depending on the grammatical gender of the noun. She's not used to making such a distinction and therefore easily gets it wrong.) Some Ojibway children of bilingual parents, then, didn't consistently differentiate *he* and *she* even if they spoke only English themselves. The first-grader's teacher, by the way, misinterpreted what was going on when she yelled at him, "Can't you see that that's a girl?!" He was as capable of telling boys from girls as any other child; he just spoke a version of English that didn't make the distinction in its pronouns. Since this feature of English was so anomalous, I heard it mostly in adults who were less fluent in English and in their younger children, in whom it disappeared over time. A few other features of Ojibway-influenced English often persisted into adulthood, however, such as treating the word *hair* as a plural ("My daughter's hair was getting too long so I cut them."). All of this was twenty years ago, however; children's speech in that community is probably very different today, because children now have parents who are for the most part native speakers of English (some of them bilingual, some not).

What Do Black English Speakers Do Differently?

Few aspects of English language variation have aroused stronger feelings than Black English (also known by other names, such as AAVE, African American Vernacular English). For African American speakers, it is often a strong badge of identity. On the other hand, white racists have described it as inferior, and even those without prejudices may assume, from lack of knowledge, that it involves "mistakes" in grammar or a lack of education. It is, however, just one more version of English, albeit one with a rich history that continues to evolve and refine itself. Black English has been studied and written about extensively; I'd particularly recommend *Black English* (Dillard 1972) for a linguistic overview and *Talkin* and *Testifyin* (Smitherman 1977) for a cultural one.

As with all versions of English, it's important to remember that Black English is cultural, not genetic; not all African Americans have features of Black English in their speech, and many use more features of Black English in some social contexts than in others. (I recently saw a movie, *New Jersey Drive*, in which teenaged African Americans, like all teenagers, spoke a distinctively more slangy language, in this case an African American version, with their peers than with their parents.)

Black English includes a pragmatic dimension (for instance, a high premium placed on verbal play), a semantic one (vocabulary items like *race man* and *signifyin*; Smitherman [1994] has compiled an extensive dictionary), a syntactic one (like rules for use of double negatives, which in Black English, as in many other varieties, are grammatically acceptable), and a phonological one. Some of the most prevalent features of Black English pronunciation, the dimension most relevant to our discussion of phonics and spelling, are:

initial /ð/ becomes /d/: them = dem
final /θ/ becomes /f/: mouth = mouf
final consonant clusters reduced: desk = des, also desks = desses
/r/ and /l/ omitted in middle and final positions: help = hep, sister =
  sistah (Smitherman 1977; Wolfram & Christian 1989)

Again, it's important to remember that these are not "flaws" or "mistakes" in English, any more than is the omission of /r/ by Bostonians or upper-class British.

African Americans are not all in agreement about what role educators should play as far as Black English is concerned. Some feel that teachers should accept it in children as it is, as part of African American culture, while others feel that schools have a responsibility to teach the "language of power." (See Delpit 1995 for a widely known discussion of the latter view.) My point here is basically a linguistic one: Black English is a variant of English like any other, not an aberration from a "standard" form.

Are Some Versions of English Better than Others?

It depends on what you mean by better. The linguistic answer is very different from the popular answer. The idea of "proper English" is widespread in our culture, and the person on the street would be likely to say that good English involves avoiding features such as the word *ain't*, double negatives, and so on. Let's look just at pronunciation. Whose pronunciation is better, a New Englander's, a Midwesterner's, or a Southerner's? Is a pronunciation, as heard on national newscasts, that doesn't have a strong regional flavor better than a more distinctive one?

Does the communication ability of particular speakers of English depend on which version of it they speak? Hardly; people within their own community understand them perfectly well, as do other people within their country and (perhaps with a bit more effort) speakers of English from other countries (and it's easier for the listener to adjust than it is for the speaker).

Are some accents of English better because they're a closer fit with spelling? No; English spelling is a pretty good but not ideal fit with all versions of the spoken language. There are some slight variations, particularly in which words are homophones for each dialect group (do you pronounce *Mary*, *marry*, and *merry* the same? how about *pen* and *pin*?), but they're minor.

Do some versions of English just *sound* better? It depends on who you ask. Most people feel that the language of their own speech community sounds best; after that, any judgments they have about other language variations depend on how they feel about the group involved. For instance, those who have a stereotyped view of Texans are likely to look down on the way they talk, while upper-class British pronunciation may be seen by Americans or Canadians as either highly proper or stuck-up, depending on how they feel about upper-class British people.

An example to put this discussion in a bit of a cross-cultural perspective: what do you think of these two different versions of British speakers saying, "A lovely hill with a clear view"?

A loovly ill with a clearr vyoo.

A luvvly hill with a cleah voo. (Andersson & Trudgill 1990)

These pronunciations from two regions of England (Lancashire and Norfolk, respectively) represent different combinations of older and newer pronunciations of four of the words involved. Which is better? Why? Here's a chart showing which pronunciations are the old ones and which the new:

	Old	New
lovely	loovly	luvvly
hill	hill	ill
clear	clearr	cleah
view	vyoo	voo

Is the older pronunciation better? Is the newer pronunciation better? (None of the seven versions of the phrase listed by Andersson and Trudgill uses either all old or all new forms.) The most common American version of the phrase would be, A *luvvly hill with a clearr vyoo*. Is this the best one? Are there any grounds for saying so other than your own ethnocentrism? Many Britons would say that the BBC pronunciation, A *luvvly hill with a cleah vyoo*, is best. Are they right?

What I'm of course trying to do with this series of rhetorical questions is challenge the idea that there's any logical reason for thinking that one set of pronunciations of English is better than another. In reality, pronunciation differences are qualitatively neutral, a result of divergent patterns of language change in groups of people that are at least somewhat geographically or socially distinct. Judgments about them are actually based (usually unconsciously) on how we feel about the speakers.

Is Language Variation Governed by Rules?

One of the stereotypes about linguistic differences attributes a psychological or even moral quality to them. Working-class speakers may be called lazy for dropping their g's when they say *wishin' and hopin'* instead of *wishing and hoping*. However, George Bush was considered to be not careless but political when he did the same, and New Englanders aren't considered lazy for droppin' their r's!

Let's look at the two versions of *-ing* endings phonetically: *hoping* is /hōpɪŋ/, while *hopin'* is /hōpɪn/. Nothin's been dropped at all! Rather, /ŋ/ has been changed to /n/ through a process of assimilation, because /n/ is closer physically to the preceding vowel than /ŋ/ is. This is natural in the less accented syllable of a two-syllable word and thus becomes a rule-governed variation (i.e, Change /ŋ/ to /n/ in an unstressed *ing* ending) rather than a "lazy" maneuver. Other words ending in *ing* don't follow this pattern: *sing* doesn't become *sin* or *dingaling* become *dinalin*. Also, have you ever noticed that many people pronounce *hoping* as *hope-een* (/hōpēn/), a pronunciation that nonetheless leaves the impression that the /g/ hasn't been "dropped"? In this case, the switch to *hopin'* would involve only a vowel change from /ē/ to /ɪ/.

If People Talk Differently, Will It Affect Their Reading and Spelling?

I hope I've convinced you by this point that no one way of pronouncing English is better than any other; the linguist Steven Pinker (1994) says that such a view is no more logical than it would be to say that "the song of the humpback whale contains several well-known errors, and monkeys' cries have been in a state of chaos and degeneration for hundreds of years" (p. 370). (Although a similar discussion of syntactic variation is beyond the scope of this book, the same arguments hold: *I ain't got none* expresses the same meaning as *I don't have any* and does it just as well. See Labov [1969], which has been reprinted in many anthologies, for one of the best-known discussions of this issue.) But for educators, there's a further issue, one of the relationship between language variation and learning to read and spell. Fortunately, we have some good empirical evidence on this point.

First, as far as reading is concerned, written language isn't a "best fit" for any single version of spoken English (Brengleman 1970), so that we all have to make slight (but very slight) adjustments when we read something written by an author whose English is different from our own. Goodman and Buck (1973) comment that when readers make miscues that reflect their own version of English in contrast to the author's, this is evidence that they have to have understood the meaning of the text. This applies equally (using their examples) to the six of twenty-one American readers producing "I switched off the *headlights* [for *headlamps*] of the car" and to the African American child who reads "a word *what* [for *that*] sounded good." Pronunciation-related miscues are even less problematic; in his extensive examination of readers' miscues, Goodman came to realize that rather than speak of what's written in the text, we need to think of a range of "expected responses" that allow for a variety of possible pronunciations based on the speech of the reader rather than a single pronunciation reflecting the language of the listener. (Imagine how offended we'd be if a British teacher considered it a reading error if an American child read *lieutenant* as *loo-tenant* rather than *leff-tenant*—and vice versa.) Therefore, in miscue analysis, it is most appropriate not to "count as a miscue any [reading] that is simply a phonological variant in the reader's dialect of the printed word or phrase" (Goodman & Buck 1973, p. 7).

Is this proof that speakers of all dialects will find English equally easy to learn to read? Not as such, but it does mean that written English represents all versions of spoken English with only minor variations, and that readers reading aloud will of course sound like themselves talking rather than the author. (In silent reading it naturally becomes even less an issue.) Phonetic differences between dialects and between spoken and written language are slight; African American readers need to learn that the word they see in print as *help* is the same one they may pronounce *hep* (a task made easier by their hearing the /l/ pronounced when they hear the word on television and elsewhere), but it's also true that readers from Boston and some from England need to learn that *park* represents *pahk*, and that all readers need to learn that *knife* represents *nife*. It simply isn't more of an issue for some readers than for others. (But see Gadsden & Wagner [1995] for lengthier discussions of these issues.)

It certainly doesn't hurt, however, for young readers to be exposed to writers who use the styles and rhythms of their own speech; just as

American children wouldn't normally be exposed only to British authors, African American children in particular should be reading authors like Lucille Clifton and Virginia Hamilton who incorporate features of Black English into their books. And if *all* North American children read such authors regularly, it would expose them to literature that is diverse not only culturally but linguistically, perhaps also laying some groundwork for the eventual destigmatization of language variation.

As for spelling, when I reviewed the available studies on language variation and spelling (many of them summarized in Wilde 1986/1987), I discovered that although young children often represent dialect features in their spelling, it's a relatively minor influence that virtually disappears by the upper elementary grades. All children need to learn that spelling is only somewhat phonetic, so that language variation is as much a nonissue for spelling as it is for reading.

Although the issues are more complicated for children who are bilingual or learning English as a second language, the principles are the same. The pronunciation of a child when she is reading in English and her spelling when she writes in English will of course be inclined to reflect the phonology of her first language. Imagine yourself learning a second language, let's say French. At first you'll read it with an English accent (and perhaps pronounce some words as if they were English, reading *femme* to rhyme with *gem* rather than *Tom*). If you invent spellings for words you don't know yet, they'll also reflect English spelling patterns, particularly when the French ones are tricky. But all of this is normal and will work itself out in time, primarily through a greater mastery of French rather than drill and practice on the points of confusion. Bilingual and ESL literacy are complex, partly because of the many variables involved (e.g., how much English does the child know? does the school have teachers or paraprofessionals who speak the child's language? is the child literate in his first language?). Some good sources of information are Edelsky (1986) for a research perspective and Freeman and Freeman (1992, 1994, 1997) for teaching ideas.

Aren't Many Spelling Problems Caused by Mispronouncing Words?

This question often comes up when I conduct workshops on spelling. For instance, when I share a writing sample with the spelling PRENOUNCED and ask why only the first vowel is misspelled, usually a teacher will suggest that if the child had *pronounced* the word correctly he would have known to use an *o*. I point out, however, that the word actually has a schwa for the first vowel, and that to use a long *o* would be an artificial pronunciation that we can probably only produce because we're good enough spellers to know that the word has an *o* in it. By contrast, the word *pronoun* does indeed have a long *o* in the first syllable, which would be far less likely to be spelled with another letter by a young writer. Saying a word with normal intonation in the context of a sentence is a good clue to its normal pronunciation, and invented spelling may well represent these normal pronunciations, not pronunciations that are artificial and hypercorrect for many versions of English, such as *Feb-ru-ary* and *hwich* for *which*. It's easier to just learn how to spell a word than to try to change your pronunciation of it to fit a spelling that would then seem more phonetic. Otherwise we'd all be saying *ka-nife* for *knife*. This is not less true for children whose pronunciations differ from those of the teacher; kids don't need to talk like you in order to be adequate spellers.

More mature spellers also can and do use the spelling of a related word to help them spell a sound whose spelling isn't obvious from its normal pronunciation. For instance, knowing *medicinal* can help you spell the second vowel in *medicine*, and knowing *medic* can help you remember that there's a *c* and not an *s* in *medicine* (or *medicine* can help you remember the *c* in *medic* if the latter is the word you don't know how to spell). But this approach has its limits. A teacher told this story about her husband, who had trouble remembering the spelling of *material*. He would say to her, "I can never remember. Does it have two *t*'s and I think it's one? Or does it have one *t* and I think it's two?" But he came to her triumphantly one day and said, "I finally figured it out. Related words are spelled alike, right? Well, *material* is obviously related to *matter*, so has two *t*'s!"

Why Do Some African Americans Say *Aks* for *Ask*?

In thinking about language variation, I found myself wondering about a particular feature that I've often heard in the speech of African Americans, the pronunciations /æks/ and /ækst/ (sometimes represented as *ax* and *axed*) for *ask* and *asked*, respectively. I was familiar with the process of metathesis, a reversing of the order of two sounds, as when children say *pasghetti* for *spaghetti*. But I wasn't sure why this particular pattern occurred in Black English and whether it appeared in other words. I was also aware that these pronunciations are somewhat stigmatized by those who consider Black English to be inferior to "standard" English. So I went to some experts. David Pesetsky, a linguist at MIT, told me about a computer listserve called the Linguist List, and I posted the following question there:

> My question is about the African American use of /æks/ and /ækst/ for *ask* and *asked*. Does this phenomenon occur only on this word? What's the reason it occurs? (E.g., is it easier to pronounce?)

I received a couple of dozen fascinating responses, which I've excerpted here. First, some respondents discussed issues of ease of pronunciation and metathesis. Alain Thomas, at the University of Guelph in Canada, said, "Yes, /ækst/ is easier to pronounce than /æskt/ because of the difficulty of uttering the /kt/ cluster in word-final position (both are voiceless stops). . . . Although /æks/ is just as easy to pronounce as /æsk/, I suspect the former is used for reasons of coherence"; that is, once you're saying *axed* for the past tense, it's logical to say *ax* for the present tense. He also pointed out that a number of present-day English words have metathesized from a different form in Old English or Middle English, such as *frist* turning into *first* and *wapse* into *wasp*. Alice Faber, at Haskins Laboratories, pointed out that changing /sk/ to /ks/ isn't a general feature of AAVE phonology. "It's specific to this word. In other words ending in *sk*, the *k* tends to be lost, so that *desk*, for example, would tend to be pronounced /dɛs/." Jan Tent, at the University of the South Pacific in Fiji, in an interesting digression, talked about the role of metathesis in slips of the pen and spoonerisms. He shared the following anecdote:

I enjoy making up spoonerisms. Many years ago I ordered a sandwich at the staff club at the university I was teaching at. I asked for a sandwich with "boast reef and pustard mickles." The lady at the counter didn't bat an eyelid and proceeded to make just what I wanted. The next day she asked me if I wanted the same "boast reef and pustard mickles." I recently went back to the staff club after an absence of five years and she was still there. She said, "Do you want a boast reef and pustard mickles sandwich?" She said this had become the standard way of referring to *roast beef* and *mustard pickles* among the staff of the club.

If a pattern of regularly changing /sk/ to /ks/ isn't what's going on, then what is? Several linguists responded that, in the words of Gillian Sankoff, from the University of Pennsylvania,

> the Oxford English Dictionary . . . tells us that Old English had two forms, *acsian* and *ascian*, the former being the literary standard until about 1600, when the latter gained the imprimatur of being the high-style variant. Specialists in AAVE agree that current African Americans who use /æks/ have *inherited* this as the base form of the verb.

Further comment came from Raj Mesthrie, at the University of Cape Town:

> *Aks* is I believe alive and well in parts of Britain and elsewhere in the world (e.g., my native dialect of South African Indian English, where it coexists with the standard form *ask*). The Old English form is *acsian* (suggesting an antecedent of *aks*); Middle English had *axian*, and I believe at least in the midlands of England *aks* is a variant.

Apparently, then, both *ask* and *aks* have been around for a long time. Why did one rather than the other turn up in Black English, and why is *aks* stigmatized? Mary Niepokuj at Purdue commented:

> I'm not absolutely sure how the word entered African American English as /æks/; my guess (but it's just a guess) might be that the

form /æks/ was the form most commonly used in the dialect of English to which the slaves were originally exposed, and it's persisted in African American English for the same sociolinguistic reasons that other features persist. I'd be inclined to treat it as a retention rather than as an innovation in African American English.

Mikael Parkvall, from Stockholm, commented that /æks/ is also common in the English of the West Indies. Sherri Condon, at the Université des Acadiens (University of Southwestern Louisiana), spoke to the issue of prestige; "the /æsk/ order was the one used in varieties that eventually acquired prestige: so it became the standard." She also used a nice analogy for talking about the assigning of higher status to one version of a language than another:

> I've found it very effective to work with the analogy that language is a living thing. Then we can observe the similarities between the variation in living things and the variation in language. The parallels are many and are illuminating, plus it clarifies nicely the difference between a descriptive approach and one which imposes a value system by treating one variety as privileged. How would a biologist respond if you asked whether crustaceans or arthropods were better?

I think the implications of the case of *aks* for educators are quite simple; this is a single word that plays only the tiniest of roles in the emerging literacy of African American children. In reading, context will make it clear that *ask* says /æks/, and in spelling, the African American child who writes AXT and the Anglo child who writes AST (which reflects the usual pronunciation of *asked* in connected speech in her community) are producing similar phonetic spellings in the same way; both of them need to learn that the word is spelled in a way that reflects the meaning units *ask* and *-ed*.

I learned a tremendous amount from this e-mail correspondence about *aks* and *akst*; it helped me realize how language, even for someone with some background in linguistics, can be far more complex than we realize. What I had thought might be a simple phonetic shift was actually the remnant of a rich history traceable back to Old English, with further roots in the history of slavery that is part of the past of most African Americans. It also reminded me once again of how valuable it is to increase our knowledge about language whenever possible; in these days of computer resources, experts can be surprisingly accessible. On that note, I'd like to mention an apropos maxim from Christ's Sermon on the Mount in Miles Coverdale's Bible, 1535 (supplied to me by Alain Thomas): "Axe and it shal be giuen you."

A final footnote to this discussion: I just saw the movie *A Time to Kill* and was struck by a powerful scene (not present in the John Grisham novel the book is based on) in which the great actor Samuel L. Jackson, playing a Mississippi working-class African American on trial for murder, challenges his lawyer to ask one of the witnesses a risky question whose answer ends up being a dramatic turning point in the trial. As his lawyer hesitates, Jackson says three times, with great force, "Ax him!" For me, the eloquence of these simple words is magnified by the knowledge that they are uttered in a language form that has often been stigmatized. Human beings are sadly still too often prone to see difference from oneself as inferiority, and teachers in particular have a great responsibility to challenge and work to eradicate this notion.

Part Two

FIVE

Skills and the Big Phonics Debate: A Whole Language, Commonsense Perspective

These days the words *phonics* and *basic skills* seem to be on everyone's tongue. In 1996, Texas, California, and Ohio considered mandating spelling books, the formal teaching of phonics, or both. Even presidential candidate Bob Dole came out in favor of spelling bees and phonics (Dole 1996). At the same time, whole language teachers continue to insist that they've always taught children how to use sound-letter relationships as part of learning how to read. (Regie Routman's 1996 book, *Literacy at the Crossroads*, is an excellent discussion of current literacy debates and the role that teachers can play in defending their practices.)

I'd like to step back a little from the form this debate most often takes—the role that phonics should play in beginning reading—and explore the broader issue of the role of "skills" in learning to read and spell. What are skills anyway? How do children acquire phonics knowledge and use it when they're learning to read and spell? Where does phonemic awareness fit in? Does phonics play a role for older children? In particular, what can and should kids do when they're reading and come to a word they don't know, or when they're writing and don't know how to spell a word? First I'll explore these issues in a general, theoretical way, then I'll focus on more specific teaching ideas, first for reading and then for spelling.

What We Talk About When We Talk About Skills

Quotes from the teachers' lounge:

- "Now that I'm using more literature, I'm still teaching skills, but in context."
- "I was really disappointed in that response guide to *Charlotte's Web*; it's just a bunch of skill and drill activities."
- "I'd like to use whole language, but I'm afraid the kids won't get the skills they need."
- "The principal's driving me crazy; all of my students are reading and writing, but he wants me to teach skills directly so that their test scores won't suffer."
- "I wish I had more time for writing, but the kids have got to get their spelling skills in somehow."
- "I'm an eclectic teacher; students need lots of rich experiences with reading and writing in context, but they need instruction in skills too."

These comments are familiar to anyone who talks with elementary school teachers about how best to encourage children's literacy development; the term *skills* is used to characterize a particular type of language curriculum (focusing on discrete elements) that's often contrasted with activities (like literature discussions or the writing process) whose focus is more global. *Skills* has also taken on a broader meaning, as an identifying term for an orientation toward literacy instruction that defines learning language as being at least somewhat a matter of acquiring individual pieces that are then combined into a larger whole (DeFord 1985). Many teachers feel reluctant to define themselves as either entirely within or entirely outside the skills camp; they view themselves as professionals who are unwilling to go to either extreme on a continuum of philosophies, choosing instead a "both-and" orientation, where the teaching of skills supplements more experiential learning and in particular provides a degree of security that all bases have been covered. Others, of course, feel that this reluctance to choose sides doesn't work, and that all instructional practices reflect an underlying theoretical base that needs to be internally consistent (Harste & Burke 1980).

The debate over "skills" can't be resolved until we look at the assumptions underlying the term, assumptions that may be promoting unwarranted beliefs and practices. Lakoff and Johnson (1980) have talked about how our thinking is often grounded in metaphor, where one concept is understood in terms of another. Sometimes a whole set of idioms grows out of a single, usually implicit metaphor, so that an underlying equation that love is a physical force, for example, finds expression in talk of relationships that have electricity, sparks, magnetism, and people gravitating to one another. Similarly, an underlying metaphor of the mind as machine may be expressed in such phrases as *the wheels are turning, I'm a little rusty,* and *we're running out of steam* (Lakoff & Johnson 1980, 27, 49). Smith (1988a) makes the case that the term *skills* suggests a metaphor of "mind as muscle":

> Traditionally . . . the word *skill* is employed with respect to physical activities, either sporting (the skills of rowing or high-jumping) or manual (the skills of carpentry or embroidery). The distinctive characteristic of all these activities is that they involve physical dexterity, or motor coordination, and frequently muscular strength as well. And it seems to me . . . that both motor coordination and muscular strength increase with exercise, drill, and practice.
>
> But cognitive abilities like reading, writing, and thinking are not the kinds of activities that improve with exercise and drill. The brain has no muscles to strengthen through repetitive activities, and no motor coordination is involved (except for physical concomitants like handwriting). When we talk about reading and writing skills we are speaking metaphorically and the metaphor can be inappropriate. (102–3)

Basal readers often have a sequence for teaching skills that looks like these "steps to develop the skills needed to read the selection": "Introduce each skill; instruct students in using it; provide guided

practice; have students summarize what they've learned; assign inde-
pendent practice" (Durr 1986, 10). These would seem to be very appropriate steps for helping learners develop many physical skills; one
can imagine their being used by a swimming teacher introducing a
new stroke, a parent teaching a child to tie shoelaces, a cooking
teacher showing how to chop onions, and so on. But would they be
applicable to a more cognitive process, like learning to prepare one's
income tax return? Most of us would approach such a task in other
ways. One person might plunge in with the tax forms, and, when
needed, refer to the manual or phone someone for advice. Another
might buy a tax preparation book and read straight through, with the
idea of spotting every possible deduction. A third might take a class,
which would probably involve lectures on both general and specific
topics, question-and-answer sessions, and perhaps some practice exercises. Someone else might choose to buy a computer tax program to
make the job easier with more automated. But it's hard to imagine
that an adult would look for a teacher who would introduce the separate subskills of using the manual's index, ordering tax forms, compil-
ing deductions, and so on, and oversee lengthy practice sessions on
each one before going on to the next.

Which example, the physical or the cognitive, is more closely al-
lied to literacy learning? Common sense suggests that it's the latter,
and I'd like to propose a moratorium on the metaphor of skills when
talking about learning to read and write. Instead, we might better use
the terms *knowledge* and *strategies* when we talk about cognitive
processes like literacy learning. Drill and practice make sense for
physical skills: all the abstract knowledge in the world can't make
you a swimmer, a shoelace tier, or an onion chopper; after someone
has shown you how, you just need to do it, and your skill increases as
a direct result of the practice.

Also, this kind of skill development doesn't involve strategies—
thinking through a range of choices. Again, when you tie your
shoes, you just do it, and don't have to think about alternatives.
(Perhaps the one area of both reading and writing that's somewhat
parallel to such physical skills is fluency in a general sense, which
presumably does improve with practice, particularly in the case of

writing (or typing), which includes a physical component.) Doing your taxes, however, clearly involves both knowledge (which income is subject to self-employment tax? how much of my interest charges can I deduct?) and strategies (what do I do when I can't understand the language of the tax manual? what's the best way to organize my receipts?).

In applying this knowledge and strategies model to literacy learning, I'll focus on two areas that are a small part of the larger reading and writing processes but a fairly large part of traditional instruction: word recognition and spelling. These are also, of course, the areas of literacy currently being debated the most hotly. Everyone agrees that kids should read good books and express themselves well in writing; the battles are over how they should approach unfamiliar words when reading and learn how to spell them when writing. These battles also extend to discussions of how children can best get to the point of being able to read and write independently.

I need to make a major point here about the term *word recognition*. Reading is not basically word recognition, it's a process of constructing meaning from text. I'm focusing in this discussion on the piece of what we call reading that involves being able to look at a word and say, That says *red*. But in normal reading we don't particularly attend to individual words; they're processed below the level of conscious awareness. When I talk about word recognition here, I'm using the term to mean whatever it is that enables us to process the "code" of written text, in one way when we're reading normally and in another way when we have to stop and puzzle over a word. But reading itself is far more than recognizing words.

Proficient readers and spellers operate most of the time out of a great deal of internalized knowledge. We know most words that we come across in our reading and know how to spell most words that we write. Beginners, with less knowledge, often need to ask themselves, What can I do when I'm reading and come across a word I don't know? What can I do when I don't know how to spell a word? As learning to read and write proceeds, readers and writers are able to recognize words and produce correct spellings more directly and automatically (i.e., below the level of conscious awareness) and have less and less need for mediating strategies (Smith 1988b). (This doesn't mean that miscues and invented spellings never occur, since factors beyond or separate from the word level are also operating, producing meaning-related mispredictions as well as slips of the pen. However, literate people *can* correctly read and spell many thousands of individual words, even out of context.) Shown diagrammatically, the process looks something like this:

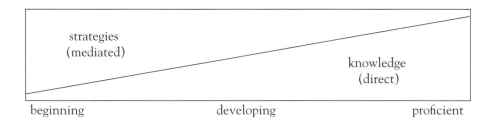

Knowledge and Strategies for Word Recognition in Reading

Traditional skills instruction in reading, typically seen in basal readers, focuses heavily on the learning and naming of words, through formal introduction of new vocabulary as well as phonics instruction. Comprehension is then treated as another skills level, which follows once the words have been decoded (Goodman, Shannon, et al. 1988). An alternative, more contemporary view regards reading as a transactional process of constructing meaning from text (e.g., Anderson et al. 1985; Rosenblatt 1978); teachers who work from this theory typically focus more on integrated experiences with complete texts. But even within such a model, we realize that proficient readers do know many individual words and can recognize them out of context (knowledge) and that it's appropriate to ask what readers can and should do when they encounter words they don't know (strategies). We therefore need to think seriously about the role of the teacher in promoting growth in both knowledge and strategies, even when speaking only of this single, narrow dimension of word recognition.

We can all think of many examples of two kinds of learning in our own lives: learning that took place with formal instruction, explicitly (even in such simple ways as a car salesperson showing you how the sunroof works), and learning that took place without conscious attention, tacitly (for instance, you can probably mentally reconstruct many of the landmarks on the route you drive to work each day even though no one "taught" them to you). This is also true of literacy learning, even though skills approaches assume that virtually everything has to be taught explicitly; the vast majority of what proficient readers know about written words is a result of tacit learning. This knowledge is of two types: recognition in print of tens of thousands of individual words, very few of which were ever presented formally by a teacher or looked up in the dictionary (Krashen 1993), and an understanding of graphophonic (letter-sound) relationships that helps us read new words and even pronounce nonsense words.

Beginning Reading

Although skills approaches assume that phonics knowledge in particular needs to be taught formally, there's a strong body of evidence that children are able to abstract it themselves from appropriate experiences with written text (Moustafa, 1993, 1995; Weaver 1988, 1990). The most important role for the teacher, therefore, is to provide the extensive experiences with written text that provide the data from which children absorb knowledge of individual words, as well as a sense of graphic patterns and graphophonic relationships.

This is very similar to the way in which children learning to talk come to know so many words and to produce all the sounds of their language; and just as spoken language must have a context to give it meaning (Wells 1986), emerging readers need external support to grasp the meaning of written language until they can interact with it more independently. One of our most important tools for doing this is predictable books (Rhodes 1981), accompanied by practices (like lap reading, big books, taped books, and dictated stories) that provide a bridge between emergent readers and simple yet meaningful, natural-language texts.

Authors such as Bobbi Fisher (1991, 1995) and Carol Avery (1993) provide portraits of how these activities are incorporated into the daily life of primary-grade classrooms. Readers move from reading simple books with external support (or through memorizing) to "really" reading them and gradually build both their knowledge and their fluency to the point where they can deal with increasingly difficult texts. In a sense, these forms of assisted reading can be called the word recognition strategies of beginning readers. How do you identify an unknown word when you aren't familiar with the written form of *most* words? Employ some combination of memorizing the text, predicting the text (through pictures, familiarity of the story, and so on), and listening to a person, live or on tape, read aloud while you're focusing on the print.

Moustafa (1993, 1995) has documented how it is exactly this kind of experience that eventually enables beginning readers to use the graphophonic system as part of how they figure out new words: reading a whole text with assistance builds the ability to recognize individual words as part of that text, which then enables children to figure out new words through analogy. For instance, a child who can read *big* and *funny* can figure out *bunny*. This is all without formal instruction in words or sounds.

To teachers versed in a skills model, it may seem counterintuitive that the transition into "real" reading could occur so informally; it's perhaps precisely because so much learning in all areas takes place without our conscious awareness of the process that we discount its extent. One way for adults to appreciate the power of incidental learning is to experience something that replicates as closely as possible the feeling of being a beginning reader. I use an activity adapted from one created by Carolyn Burke, in which a familiar fairy tale text is transcribed in an unfamiliar alphabet. The first page (of 25) reads, "The Three Little Pigs. Once upon a time there were three little pigs. One day the three little pigs left home. Each little pig wanted to build a house," and looks like this (an appropriate picture is included):

$$+\infty\theta \quad +\infty \div\theta\theta \quad \Sigma\&++\Sigma\theta \quad \cap\&\partial\approx$$
$$\Omega\Gamma\yen\theta \quad >\cap\Omega\Gamma \quad \cent +\&\pi\theta \quad +\infty\theta\div\theta$$
$$\equiv\theta\div\theta \quad +\infty\div\theta\theta \quad \Sigma\&++\Sigma\theta \quad \cap\&\partial\approx.$$
$$\Omega\Gamma\theta \quad \pi\cent\# \quad +\infty\theta \quad +\infty\div\theta\theta \quad \Sigma\&++\Sigma\theta$$
$$\cap\&\partial\approx \quad \Sigma\theta\Omega+ \quad \infty\Omega\pi\theta. \quad \theta\cent\yen\infty$$
$$\Sigma\&++\Sigma\theta \quad \cap\&\partial \quad \equiv\cent\Gamma+\theta\pi \quad +\Omega \quad \pounds>\&\Sigma\pi$$
$$\cent \quad \infty\Omega>\approx\theta.$$

We discuss the story, talk about the pictures, and read chorally; the readers are invited to chime in with me as they follow the text visually. Partway through the highly repetitive story, not only are the readers able to read together largely without my input (which could possibly be explained as prediction or memorization), but they've also acquired a few sight words and are even recognizing individual letters, as well as finding the process as a whole to be comfortable and enjoyable.

Although this isn't an exact parallel to what beginning readers experience (since these adults do already know how to read), the process is still a powerful demonstration of how much can be learned without explicit instruction in a very brief time. (I usually also do parallel activities with lessons from two basal readers, one sight-word based and the other phonics based, both using the same altered alphabet. The contrast is striking, in both ability to read the text and the students' emotional response.)

Although much of readers' knowledge about words and phonics emerges through reading, it also makes sense to include a limited amount of more formal instruction, but in a way that works inductively from what children already know. A contextualized focus on learning new words as part of vocabulary and concept development can certainly include exposure to the written forms of those words. (For instance, the teacher might help a group of beginning readers produce a wall chart listing all the animals they can think of.) Teachers can provide contextualized activities for learning the alphabet if children don't already know it when they begin school (see McGee & Richgels 1989 for suggestions), as well as activities using literary devices like alliteration and rhyme to highlight patterns of beginning, medial, and ending sounds (Weaver 1990). Word families like *bat, cat, rat* can similarly be explored. Mills, O'Keefe, and Stevens (1992) present a rich description of how explorations of phonics can be integrated into a varied classroom literacy program, as do the Fisher and Avery books I mentioned earlier. Invented spelling also plays a role in developing phonics knowledge, as we'll see in a bit. These suggestions may seem like a shockingly small amount of instruction to replace the many hours of phonics skill instruction in basal readers, but phonics is a far more powerful tool when considered as part of a repertoire of strategies than as a collection of skills.

Phonemic Awareness

There's been a good deal of discussion about phonemic awareness in the past several years, some of it prompted by Marilyn Adams's book *Beginning to Read* (1990). *Phonemic awareness* is defined as the knowledge that words can be broken down into discrete units of sound, as well as the ability to manipulate those sounds. Adults who are literate in alphabetic languages tend to have phonemic awareness, while those literate in nonalphabetic languages like Chinese tend not to (Read, Yun-Fei, Hong-Kin, and Bao-Qing 1986). Examples of tasks directed at developing phonemic awareness might include reading children three words, such as *cot*, *pot*, and *hat*, and asking them which one has a different sound (in the middle, in this case) from the other two, or asking them to say *park* and then ending it with /t/ instead of /k/ (Juel, Griffith & Gough 1986).

A number of studies have shown that children with phonemic awareness are more likely to be successful in learning to read. For instance, a longitudinal study by Juel, Griffith, and Gough (1986) found that children without phonemic awareness weren't very likely to be good readers by the end of first grade. In my opinion, these findings are reasonable. But the real issue is how to help children develop phonemic awareness. Philip Gough (e-mail communication 1996) has suggested that the kindergarten curriculum should include phonemic awareness training, and there are published programs that feature decontextualized activities for blending individual phonemes into words and identifying the position of a given phoneme in a word.

However, any teacher of young children who works with invented spelling knows that young children's spelling shows that they have phonemic awareness. They usually begin by representing initial sounds, then start representing all the consonants, and eventually include the vowels. An invented spelling like WUN for *one* would be impossible without phonemic awareness, and invented spelling eventually gets sophisticated enough to represent phonemes like the /n/ in *went* (which stands out less than the /n/ in *when*).

Given that children's phonemic awareness is evident in their invented spelling, that the vast majority of children pick up invented spelling easily, and that invented spelling has the further benefit of enabling children to write from an early age, there's no reason to put all children through a formal phonemic awareness training program. (Informal activities that promote phonemic awareness, such as playing around with rhyme and alliteration and playing games ["I spy something that starts like . . .", for example] aren't objectionable since they are fun and worth doing for their own sake.) Although a number of studies have documented the effectiveness of phonemic awareness training (some of them are summarized in Adams 1990), it seems that a convincing case for it could only be made by measuring its effects in contrast to those of a strong writing program based on invented spelling, since invented spelling not only promotes and demonstrates phonemic awareness but has many other benefits.

How to Figure Out Unfamiliar Words

Strategies for reading a word that you don't recognize are learned by reading books that are appropriately difficult; that is, they contain some unfamiliar words but not so many that the flow of comprehensible reading is lost. (No reader should have to puzzle over every third or even every tenth word.) Once a developing reader is regularly reading in this way, one of the tasks she faces (always as part of the larger task of creating meaning) is how to deal with unfamiliar words as the meaning of a text evolves.

An unfamiliar word may be one from the reader's oral vocabulary that she doesn't recognize in print or (more likely with more proficient readers) one that isn't known at all. Proficient readers may choose to skip over an unfamiliar word, look it up, try different pronunciations to see if it's a known word, or ask someone, but perhaps the most common strategy is to read the word (with or without pronouncing it mentally) without much sense of its meaning but realizing that in future encounters it'll seem more familiar until it's finally understood. (Nagy, Herman & Anderson [1985] have demonstrated that new vocabulary is indeed learned by this type of incremental process.)

I'd like to suggest a model for developing word recognition strategies in the context of reading that is a reasonable approximation of what fluent readers do. In this model, children, through a series of informal minilessons or discussions, can be helped to become aware of both the strategies they've already developed on their own and how to supplement them with new ones.

A reader who is generally comprehending a text but encounters an unknown word has a variety of possible options that can be placed in a sequential paradigm (Figure 5–1). Problems of comprehension are beyond the scope of this discussion, but it should be noted that readers should rarely if ever be reading texts so difficult that this type of mediated word identification needs to be practiced more than occasionally. (I'm not suggesting that proficient readers necessarily follow such a sequence, merely that one can be constructed as a scaffold for developing readers. Also, these are strategies to use only when the reader's own flow of meaning construction is disrupted, not for every unknown word or miscue.) At every point in this sequence, the reader asks whether the strategy has been successful. If so, no further strategies are necessary; if not, he can either move on to the next strategy or decide that knowing the word doesn't matter enough to be worth the effort involved (with either choice seen as legitimate).

The first step in the sequence is to decide to skip the word altogether, guess the meaning ("it's some kind of flower"), or use a mental placeholder such as "blank" or "something" in its place. Since any single word is usually relatively unimportant to the meaning of a text as a whole, this is often the best choice for keeping the flow of reading going. Also, reading on will frequently provide enough further information that the word will fall into place in retrospect (often by the end of the sentence). However, if the word is important to the meaning, or if the reader would just like to know what it is, he can go on to other strategies.

For a developing reader whose knowledge about graphophonic

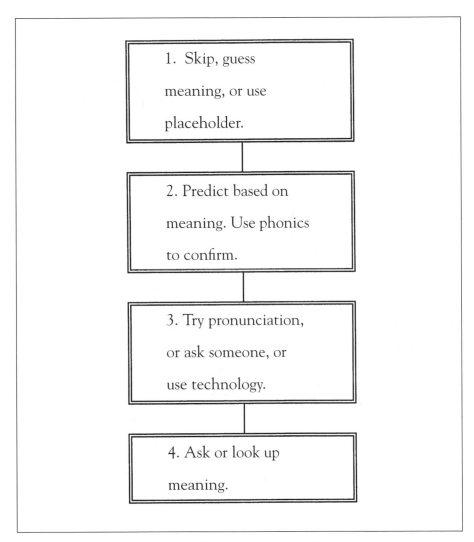

FIG 5–1   *Strategies for dealing with an unknown word in reading*

relationships isn't complete enough to look at a word and immediately come up with a reasonable pronunciation of it, a good choice at this point is to predict a couple of possible words based on meaning and initial letter, then use phonics to confirm whether any of them is correct. This strategy can be developed in a minilesson using a *cloze* (fill-in-the-blank) technique. For instance, students are presented

with the sentence, My favorite animal at the zoo was the c_____.
After they make guesses like *cheetah, chimpanzee, cat, camel,* and so
on, the rest of the word is uncovered and the students are asked to
explain how they now know it is one of these words and not another
(e.g., I see an *m* and an *l,* so it looks like *camel* and not *cheetah.*) After
this process has become familiar, an example that students are unlikely to recognize (e.g., *coatimundi*) can point out that this strategy
may only serve to disconfirm your predictions rather than provide a
definitive answer.

The next strategy, if the previous one doesn't work, is to focus
more closely on the word in order to produce a reasonable pronunciation for it and then see if that rendition is a word that you recognize
and that fits the context. There are three variations. First, the reader
can try to figure out the word herself, attempting a few reasonable
pronunciations. Don't suggest that children sound out a word letter
by letter; it's better to ask a group to look at the word globally and
suggest what it might be based on the letters it includes or on a possible word they already know that looks like it. (Displaying the word
with the vowels replaced by asterisks while doing this exercise is a
way to avoid short-circuiting the process with a too-quick right answer, as well as focusing attention on the more useful consonant letters, which you can also suggest that students do when they are
reading themselves.) The second way to come up with the pronunciation of a word is, of course, to ask someone. A third choice has just
recently become technologically possible: there are now hand-held
spell-checkers that pronounce words orally after they've been typed
in. Although they're currently a little expensive (close to $100),
these devices may eventually eliminate any argument that phonics is
needed for words that aren't recognizable from context.

I've intentionally omitted the dictionary as a resource at this
point in the process, when the reader is focusing mainly on producing an oral rendition of the word to find out if it's a familiar one. Dictionary pronunciation guides are difficult to decipher even for adults,
let alone young readers. The dictionary is more useful to proficient
readers, who can recognize most words that they know and would
look up a word mainly to get its meaning.

Once the reader has been able to come up with an oral version of a word, if it's one that she doesn't recognize as part of her vocabulary, she can either decide she's gained enough of its meaning from the context to continue reading or choose to try to find out the meaning more precisely, the obvious courses of action being to ask someone or to look the word up in either a standard or an electronic dictionary. (She may discover at this point that she does indeed know the word but didn't recognize it because she mispronounced it.)

I wouldn't describe any of the above as skills; they're strategy choices that involve underlying knowledge about such features as sound-letter relationships and dictionary layout. Since the focus is on building the learner's network of strategies rather than on teaching a sequence of skills, it's appropriate if not essential to begin developing these strategies through exploring the children's existing word-identification schemata. You might begin an introductory minilesson by asking children to talk about what they do when they come to a word they don't know and then move, as a first step, into the pros and cons of skipping words, discussing other strategies in later lessons. After each minilesson, ask the children to try out their new strategy ideas in their reading and report back on how they worked.

It's important to note the minimal role of phonics in this process; it's used mainly as adults use it: to confirm or disconfirm predictions and as a way of determining in a global (rather than letter-by-letter) sense what a word might be. Since less mature readers' knowledge of phonics is less elaborate than that of proficient readers, they'll be less successful in using this cueing system. (However, we're talking here about children who have a strong enough sense of the "cipher" [Juel, Griffith & Gough 1986] that they can read nonsense words. Children who aren't at this point yet need to be doing more assisted reading.) Rather than attempting to compensate for children's limited phonics knowledge by teaching them every possible rule (rules that are of limited usefulness anyway: Smith 1988b), why not instead spend the time on reading, so that children can induce phonics knowledge and learn new words (in both cases, without instruction) while their attention is focused on and their minds developed by the pleasures of story?

Some children may, of course, need more individual help in

71

developing and integrating their knowledge and strategies related to reading words. Haussler (1984) has documented how a small proportion of emergent readers go off track by overfocusing or underfocusing on print (i.e., "sounding out" with a disregard for preserving meaning or continuing merely to retell a story from pictures and memory without really reading). The same kinds of patterns can be seen in developing readers (where an underfocus on print may take the form of predicting a word but not checking to see if the prediction is confirmed by the print) and may not always be changed as a result of mere discussion of strategies. Reading Recovery (Clay 1979; DeFord, Lyons & Pinnell 1991; Pinnell 1989) is one possible model for working with such children, helping them interact with text simple enough to draw on their existing knowledge as well as providing a more personalized focus on practice with a repertoire of strategies.

Research Support for Not Teaching Phonics

Rather than attempt to review all the research about the effects of phonics and draw a single conclusion from a large number of studies with different methodologies and theoretical orientations, I'll focus on just a few pieces of evidence: one experimental study, two extensive comparative studies, and one review of much of the literature in the field.

First, Moustafa (1995) showed that children can read new words on the basis of words they already know, without formal instruction about sounds and letters. First graders who recognized a number of common words were successfully able to read pseudowords formed by recombining parts (technically, onsets and rimes) of the known words. (For instance, parts of *brown* and *just* were combined to make *brust*.) Moustafa described this process as occurring through children's "natural ability to make analogies [across] print words" (473).

Second, Dahl and Freppon (1995) conducted extensive quantitative and qualitative studies of children in eight kindergarten and first-grade classrooms, two skills-based and two whole language each. (The same children were followed for two grades.) Children in both types of classrooms were similar in quantitatively measured learning outcomes; in particular, their knowledge of the alphabetic principle as determined from their spelling was similar, although only the skills-based classrooms included formal phonics instruction and worksheets. The children in whole language classrooms, however, showed more of a sense of ownership of literacy (which was achieved only by the most proficient learners in the skills-based classrooms).

Third, Manning, Manning, and Long (1989, 1990) studied inner-city children in whole language and skills-oriented programs from kindergarten to the end of second grade and found that the children from whole language classrooms were better at both reading and spelling, the latter even though the skills classrooms had a formal spelling program in first and second grade. The children in the whole language classrooms not only were stronger readers generally but were more proficient on tasks involving words and parts of words.

It should be noted that both the Dahl and Freppon and the Manning et al. studies involved whole language classrooms, while many other comparative studies have contrasted a phonics approach with a sight-word methodology. Turner (1989), our fourth example, examined a large number of studies largely of that type that had been used to support arguments for or against phonics. His conclusions are worth quoting at length:

> Systematic phonics falls into that vast category of weak instructional treatments with which education is perennially plagued. Systematic phonics appears to have a slight and early advantage over a basal-reader/whole-word approach as a method of beginning reading instruction. . . . However, this difference does not last long and has no clear meaning for the acquisition of literacy in the [larger] sense. . . . Moreover, learning theory offers little reason to believe that it should do so. (283)

In my opinion, the most important question is always, Are these children, in my classroom, learning to read? But there is also strong research support for the position that formal phonics instruction doesn't need to be a part of what goes on in primary-grade classrooms.

73

Spelling Knowledge and Strategies

Spelling knowledge, like word knowledge for reading, consists of two parts: being able to spell individual words and knowing enough about graphophonic relationships to produce reasonable spellings for words you don't know. (Phonics knowledge also presumably helps you remember the spellings of the individual words.)

At the word level (i.e., writing a word one knows how to spell), this knowledge is quite close to that used in reading (though you have to know a word better to spell it than you do to read it).

When focusing on sounds and letters, however, the relationship between reading and spelling isn't reciprocal in the same way, since sounds and letters don't match up one-to-one. Each spoken word in the language has a written form; this is part of a larger pattern in which letters can be described in terms of their possible pronunciations and those sounds in turn in terms of their possible spellings. For instance:

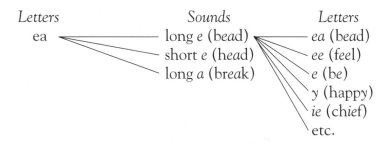

These relationships are so complex that it would be quite a task to teach them explicitly, but the process of children's inventing their own spellings is a way in which they can teach themselves about phonics and, particularly if given appropriate guidance, come to terms over time with its complexity.

Beginning invented spellers, working from their knowledge of letter names, often appear to be asking themselves, What (single) letter spells each of these sounds? They then produce one-letter-per-phoneme spellings such as BADR (butter), LIK (like), and NE (knee). (I have a writing sample from a first grader who wrote both

LIK for *like* and LIX for *likes*, the latter making use of a letter-name that actually includes two consonant sounds [i.e., /ks/].) As children mature as spellers, however, they realize that sounds can be spelled in more than one way and often need more than one letter, so that one sees invented spelling like CIEK for *kick* (exploring different ways to represent /k/), and PANTE for *paint* (using a silent final *e*). As this capacity develops, teachers not only expose children to more words through reading and encourage more proofreading as they write, but also ask questions like, What other ways could you spell that word (or sound)? and, Does that spelling look like the word you have in mind?"

Chomsky (1971) was the first to suggest that spelling, rather than reading, is the appropriate arena for children to focus on phonics relationships, and that they'll do so naturally since the problem they spontaneously set for themselves is, How do I represent this sequence of sounds in writing? (By contrast, young readers tend to focus more on meaning, as we see in their holistic retelling of texts; they shift their attention to the graphophonic level, with its resultant distraction, only when necessary [Bissex 1980].)

As children think (by their own choice) about the kinds of patterns that occur in our spelling system, instruction can, inductively, help them make some of this knowledge more conscious. For instance, a minilesson might guide children to think of all the different ways that long *a* is spelled in words they know, as well as which spellings are the most common ones and therefore the most reasonable predictions when writing an unknown long-*a* word. (See Wilde 1992 for extensive suggestions for such lessons.)

Since given the nature of our spelling system any word in English could be spelled in several reasonable ways, writers have to know the spelling of many individual words to be effective (i.e., not merely phonetic) spellers. (Graphophonic knowledge is often more helpful as an aid to remembering a correct spelling once it's known than it is to producing it in the first place. Even the relatively consistent "*i* before *e*" rule can only tell us that *chief* isn't spelled *cheif*, but not that it's not spelled *cheef* or *cheafe*.) Writers must therefore also be readers, and will learn the spellings of many words incidentally, through reading. Some writers are more successful than others at picking up spellings from reading, a difference that occurs even among proficient readers and that persists into adulthood. This may be out of a general focus on visual information that comes naturally to some people but not others; good spellers are often those for whom a single misspelled word on a restaurant menu "leaps out," without conscious effort. Those who aren't naturally good spellers can learn to produce more polished texts through a solid repertoire of strategies.

Before moving on to strategies, however, we should mention the skills approach to spelling seen in textbooks. Although these texts don't usually use the term *skills* as incessantly as basal readers do, they typically concentrate on small pieces of language: the spellings of individual words, and patterns for spelling individual phonemes. Thus a lesson objective might be to "spell words in which /ē/ is spelled *ee* and *ea*." As this example indicates, the major emphasis is on words themselves, with an awareness of graphophonic patterns as a secondary consideration (since such patterns can't, of course, predict correct spellings definitively).

In this context, perhaps the most important criticism of spelling books is that their focus is so narrow, particularly given the amount of time spent with them. In most classrooms that use them, spelling books occupy at least fifteen minutes a day (and often much more), yet all they accomplish is to teach children a few words a week (since they already know an average of about 65 percent of the words before studying them [Stetson & Boutin 1980]) and focus some of their attention on spelling patterns without developing it to the level of predictive strategies. (See Wilde 1990 for a more extensive critique of spelling books.) Strategies in a broader sense are largely unaddressed, so that the issue of what to do when you want to write a word you don't know how to spell is never explored, nor are such related issues as how to make sure that a job application letter is perfectly spelled. The few exceptions are some useful but decontextualized dictionary lessons, as well as proofreading exercises that are so artificial as to be likely to be more harmful than helpful; see Wilde (1990) for a further discussion of these.

Spelling Camp

As I was working on this chapter, I got a call from Bill Graves, the education reporter for my local newspaper, the Portland *Oregonian*. He wanted my reaction to a summer camp being put on by the Riggs Institute, a phonics-oriented education company, where seventeen students ranging in age from seven to twenty-seven were studying spelling (along with some penmanship and grammar) every morning for four weeks, at a cost of $360 (see Graves 1996). In this sixty hours of class time, students learn seventy phonograms (spelling patterns like *au*) and twenty-nine spelling rules (e.g., *sh* is "used at the beginning of a word, at the end of a syllable, but not at the beginning of any syllable after the first one, except for the ending -*ship*"—so much for *aftershave, aftershock, ashore, bloodshed, buckshot, clamshell, enshrine, eyeshade, foreshadow, gearshift, gumshoe, handshake, misshapen, moonshine, nightshade, nightshirt, outshine, pawnshop, peashooter, plowshare, reshape, spreadsheet, troubleshoot,* and *unshackle* [not to mention *mishap* and *hogshead!*]. After quoting a comment from me about the value of invented spelling, Graves reported that students at the spelling camp are required to give up invented spelling and are also expected to give up comics, television, computer games, and movies.

Clearly this is an extremely intensive approach to spelling. Even traditionalists recommend only about an hour a week of spelling instruction (Fitzsimmons & Loomer 1978), which is equivalent to about thirty-five hours in an entire regular school year. This spelling camp is perhaps a reflection of the polarized nature of much of the current debate about literacy in the eyes of the general public. Perhaps I'm wrong and this is only about parents' wanting their kids to spell. But if we understand the process of learning to spell, there's no reason why parents who merely want their children to spell better should feel compelled to send them to, as these students call it, "spelling boot camp." When parents are led to believe, however, against all reasonable interpretation of the evidence, that schools don't teach kids to spell anymore (a cry that's been taken up by Rush Limbaugh and others), their reaction is perhaps understandable. I find myself wondering how spelling has come to be seen as something that should involve so much time—and I find myself wishing that the kids at spelling camp were off swimming and hiking at some other kind of camp!

Spelling Strategies

Spelling, like word identification in reading, can be supported by a variety of strategies. As with reading, where one can either be satisfied with a placeholder or substitution or choose to aim for the exact word, a speller can either choose to invent or attempt to produce the correct spelling. These strategies can also be arranged in a paradigm (Figure 5–2), with the ordering in this case representing not so much a temporal sequence as levels of sophistication of the learner and/or the result. (This paradigm builds on an earlier and lengthier discussion of spelling strategies in Wilde 1989.)

Beginning spellers who have been encouraged to write on their own are likely to use either placeholder spelling (essentially letter strings that don't attempt very strongly if at all to represent the sounds of the word) or, increasingly, phonetic inventions like one-letter-per-phoneme spelling. As spellers mature, their strategies will begin to incorporate (consciously or not) such questions as, How have I seen this sound spelled? and, What do I know, or think I know, about the meaning of this word? (My favorite example of an adult use of this strategy came from a loan officer who, while on the telephone confirming my employment, wrote on my application that my university appointment was a "10-year [i.e., tenure] track position"!)

As writers begin to concern themselves more with producing a correctly spelled final product, they learn to apply a range of strategies that draw on their own increasing capabilities. They may, for instance, try a few ways of writing a word and see which one looks right (a common adult strategy), they may ask someone for the spelling or discuss it with her, or they may use written texts such as dictionaries, word charts on the wall, and so on. (If the teacher makes a decision

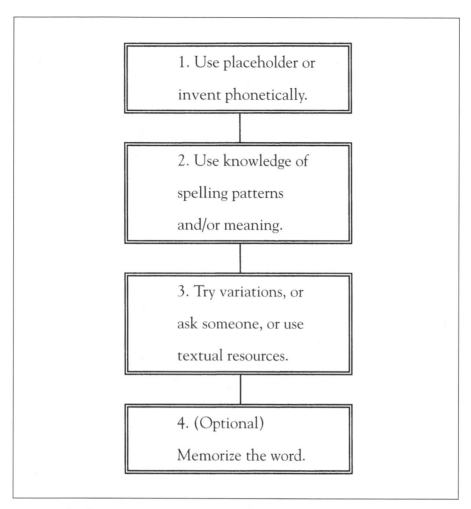

FIG 5–2   *Spelling strategies*

not to be a spelling resource for children except in special cases, it'll create a useful vacuum in which all these other strategies can develop, as well as eliminate a dependency that can delay growth in self-reliance.) Finally, an optional fourth strategy is for children to choose to memorize some words, particularly those they use often and don't seem to be picking up through incidental learning.

What's the teacher's role in this strategy development? Just as with word-identification strategies, young spellers can be encouraged to think about what they already do when trying to figure out how to spell words they don't know by heart and then helped to expand their choices, with new knowledge introduced where appropriate, as in understanding dictionary conventions. The first two strategies are especially appropriate for younger spellers who don't know a lot of words, since they're fast. The second two are more accurate and can be increasingly used as spellers mature. A class might decide together if it would be useful for everyone to work on memorizing perhaps three to five self-selected words each week. (An extensive discussion of how to build spelling strategies appears in Wilde 1992.)

Reading and Spelling Without "Skills"

As children develop their knowledge of the words they read and write and the strategies they use to supplement their knowledge, reading and writing will come to reinforce each other. Words that are seen in print will begin to appear as correct spellings, while thinking about how to represent particular sounds will build a consciousness of graphophonic relationships that supports the reading process. Reading and invented spelling therefore mesh nicely to provide two kinds of knowledge about the written forms of words: individual words are learned largely (and unconsciously) through reading, while phonics generalizations are strengthened through trying them out in writing. An approach like this one, which focuses on acquiring a great deal of knowledge primarily through tacit learning and on developing a repertoire of strategies through discussion and use, is very different in orientation and practice from a skills approach, whose central concern is the explicit teaching of small pieces. (I mean specifically basal readers and spelling textbooks, which are the type of skills programs used most often in elementary schools.)

Skills approaches assume that literacy is the sum total of skills that must be taught explicitly and that must be in large part repeated from one grade to the next. It's not stated this baldly in the textbooks themselves, but the way that they are set up makes it clear that it is an underlying assumption.) These programs therefore often provide instruction about content that children already know. (K. Goodman et al. 1988 describe some historical reasons for this design.) The instruction is typically didactic rather than discovery-oriented. By contrast, the knowledge and strategies approach proposed here realizes that knowledge about the piece of literacy that involves graphophonic relationships and the written form of individual words will largely be learned incidentally and that the role of instruction is primarily to help children develop strategies and integrate their existing knowledge. The parts of curriculum that don't directly involve the teacher—children teaching themselves through lots of reading and writing—is also crucial.

The ways in which students spend their time and are evaluated also differ in the two approaches. Skills programs typically use worksheets or other kinds of focused practice as a follow-up to instruction, with the idea that skills are reinforced through repetition. Each skill is then evaluated on the basis of performance on the worksheet and/or on tests of similar format. (Durkin [1978–1979], in a study of comprehension instruction, has suggested that such evaluative activities often *replace* instruction.) A more holistic approach realizes that both knowledge and strategies need to develop in context and are best evaluated that way, through conferences, portfolios, and so on (see Goodman, Goodman & Hood 1989). In skills programs, success is measured through repeated, narrow looks at one item at a time, while success in a whole language approach emphasizing knowledge and strategies is measured as globally as possible: that is, through such questions as, How well does this child negotiate text as a reader and construct meaning as a writer?

Are "skills" really skills at all? The term implies a generalized capability to perform some action or process, but I think that textbooks use the term as a misleading name for factual knowledge, much of it of a low level. Although skill objectives aren't stated in behavioral terms as often as they used to be, doing so might illuminate how limited in scope they really are. For instance, an objective like "[the child will be able to] spell words in which /ē/ is spelled *ee* and *ea*" is typically judged by whether students can spell twenty such words on a test. Is this any more a skill than listing the fifty states from memory would be? It seems that both clearly involve recall of factual knowledge, not skills at all.

Similarly for reading, students who have just been taught the fact that the letters *qu* typically stand for a particular sound may be asked to circle pictures that correspond to *qu* words, applying their (presumably) new knowledge in a highly restricted context but without any attempt to fit this "skill" into the larger reading process, other than as another single piece of knowledge about phonics. By contrast, an anticipated outcome for a strategy lesson might be that children will, after a minilesson exploring spellings for long *e*, be able to generate several possible spellings of a long-*e* word as they are editing a story and use their own visual sense or a resource like the dictionary to discover which one is correct (although this would probably not be stated as a required activity for all children, and would be monitored informally, perhaps through conferencing).

I haven't used the word *skills* in its traditional sense when I talk with teachers for some years now, since it carries so many unproven assumptions and misleading implications. The meaning of the whole language movement in literacy education, which looks at language learning in a highly holistic way, has been distorted by those who misunderstandingly speak of it as merely a way to teach "skills in context" (Edelsky, Altwerger & Flores 1990), and many teachers have been forced to go on the defensive, asked to prove that skills aren't suffering in their rich literacy environments. Perhaps the time has come to redefine the terms of the debate, and to ask proponents of skills programs about how they are defining, developing, and evaluating children's knowledge and strategies. Maybe we should listen more closely to the voices in the teachers' lounge saying, "My kids are picking up a lot of knowledge about phonics from their invented spelling," and, "It's nice to see the students using the same strategies that I do when they read."

SIX

What Does Invented Spelling Tell Us About Kids' Knowledge of Phonics? (And What Should We Do About It?)

Now that you're a phonics expert, how can it help you as a teacher? As we've seen from our discussion of the larger issues of teaching phonics and spelling, you're not going to use it to plan an extensive, formal phonics curriculum. (Kids don't need to be taught what a schwa sound is.) But knowing something about phonics can help you be a powerful kidwatcher, as you assess the knowledge that children show when they read and spell. And once you understand what children are doing, you're in a position to support that learning effectively, monitor their future growth, communicate with parents, and (very important) avoid wasting time on instruction they don't need or won't benefit from.

In discussing invented spelling in this chapter and miscues in the next, I go to the source—children's writing and reading—to explore a number of common patterns, what they mean, and what (if anything) we should do about them. Children are powerful informants once we have the linguistic background to interpret what they're doing with the sound-letter relationships of written English. Knowing the kinds of spelling and miscue patterns that frequently occur is also a powerful tool; many times I've been asked whether a particular child's invented spelling indicates a learning disability or even a hearing or speech problem when its features are completely normal and occur developmentally in most young spellers. Sometimes these children are older ones whose literacy achievement is behind that of other children in their class; a fifth-grade teacher may not be aware of the spelling patterns typical of second graders that are turning up in a few of her students. Similarly, teachers may assume that a particular child's miscue signifies a problem with a specific letter-sound relationship when in fact many readers make the same miscue at that point in the text, showing that there is something about the text that prompts the miscue. Let's let some children show us, through their invented spelling, what they know about written language. I'm going to illustrate each spelling pattern with a writing sample that highlights the pattern, sometimes pointing out other interesting features of the sample (since there's always a lot going on in any piece of writing). I've arranged them roughly in order of development.

Very Young Writers

When children are first learning to write, they explore some of the basic general features of written language, such as spacing between words and the direction in which print is oriented.

Words Run Together with No Spaces

Nat's picture captions (Figure 6–1) read, "This is a butterfly drinking nectar out of a flower," "A caterpillar wearing boots," and "This is a butterfly flying to the sky," and "Caterpillar." He hasn't spaced between words, although he did break his text in the two butterfly captions when he ran out of room and had to move to a new line. Is spacing between words even a phonics issue, since the spaces between words are silent? Yes and no. I think it makes most sense to think of spaces as part of the punctuation system, which is similar to the spelling system but has a much looser relationship between the spoken and the written. Periods, for instance, don't correspond consistently to any single feature of speech (they don't always signal a long pause), and punctuation marks like quotes and parentheses really have no oral equivalent at all. Punctuation represents grammar more than sound, marking off syntactic units like phrases and clauses.

In spoken language, words don't have pauses between them, so that in some ways it's amazing that children learn where to put spaces

FIG 6–1   *Nat's piece: "This is a butterfly"*

at all, even once they've realized from exposure to books that text isn't written allruntogether. They gain control of this aspect of writing fairly early because of the psychological reality of words as discrete units. Part of our understanding of language is the knowledge that even though we speak in a largely uninterrupted stream, we can abstract individual words (in fact, much of very young children's speech is made up of utterances of just one or two words). That the spaces in writing reflect this reality rather than the steady phonetic stream is just another convention that children need to learn.

If we take a closer look at Nat's writing, we realize that he's on the way to acquiring the convention; the butterfly caption line breaks occur not just where he happened to run out of room but between words. (Look at *drinking*, where he squeezed in the *n*.) Learning about word spacing generally doesn't need formal instruction; it emerges through experience with reading and writing. Nevertheless, teachers whose students are at this level might want to have an informal discussion with them about the white spaces in text and what they think about them. Nat's spelling, by the way, is very strong for a child who doesn't show letter spacing yet. He represents almost every phoneme except for consonant blends and uses *w* to represent the glided rounded vowels in *out* (OWT), *flower* (FAWR), and *to* (TAW).

Mirror Writing

Evan's piece (Figure 6–2), written on a napkin, is a little challenging to read but surprisingly logical when you've figured it out. If you start with the third letter in the second line and read backward, going up to the first line and then back down to the second, you'll see that it says *chicken wings with rice with brown rice* (HGN WNGZ WT RIS WF BRAN RIS).

Mirror writing and reversals (a visual rather than phonetic aspect of language) are among the features of developmental spelling most misunderstood by the general public (and in some cases teachers). Reversals have become so strongly associated with dyslexia (whether accurately so or not is another discussion) that they're seen by nonspecialists as a diagnostic marker. But reversals are completely normal in children learning to write. Typically, directionality in early writing is flexible, since children haven't yet learned that it matters, and a

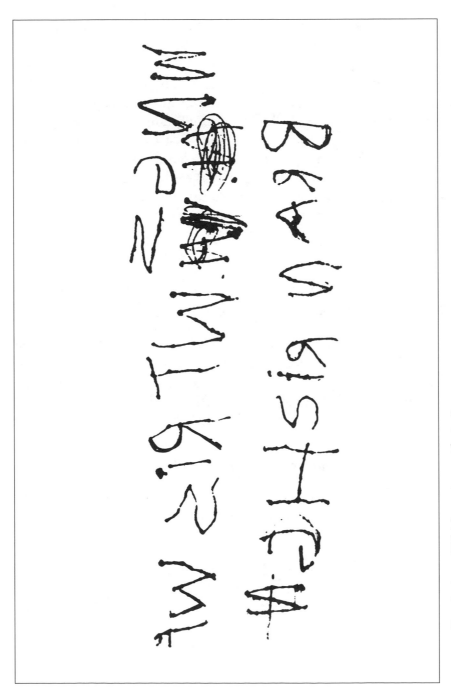

FIG 6–2 *Evan's piece: "Chicken wings with rice"*

word doesn't seem particularly more "backward" to them than a drawing of a cat facing to the left does.

Evan is at this point developmentally, yet interestingly—and typically—his letters for the most part are consistent in their directionality, so that the writing is almost a perfect mirror image, except for the s in *rice* in the bottom line and what's presumably a reversed (in relation to the other letters) z in *wings*. (I'm guessing that the last letter in *rice* in the top line was meant to be an s, but z is plausible too.) One of Evan's spellings is particularly interesting; why is *chicken* HGN? The name of the letter h (/āč/) contains the /č/ sound that's the first sound of *chicken*, and Evan's G (/g/) is the voiced equivalent of the /k/ sound in the word.

Once directionality in general gets straightened out (as documented by Clay 1975), children often still reverse a few letters. When older children (third grade or so) are reversing, there's usually one of two reasons: either the child is less mature as a writer generally (see Terry's piece in Figure 6–23 later in this chapter) or she's having trouble remembering the orientation of a letter or two (typically b and d). One of the simplest ways to deal with the latter is to sit down with the child and help her think of a quick way to remember. One of the easiest is to write the word *bed* on a slip of paper and point out that when the letters are facing the right way it looks like a bed. (She might want to tape the slip of paper on her desk to help her remember.)

Learning to Represent Sounds

Once children have begun using invented spelling in earnest, they spend a lot of time and intellectual energy exploring how to represent particular sounds.

Letter-Name Spellings

Young spellers who aren't yet always representing vowels will often use a single letter to represent a whole syllable; Anna used this strategy both for .E.T., which is the same as the standard spelling (except for the periods) and for .R.K., her charming spelling of *arcade* (Figure 6–3). Barbara, writing about a robber who stole not only the TV but the VEASYARE (Figure 6–4), has moved beyond a letter-

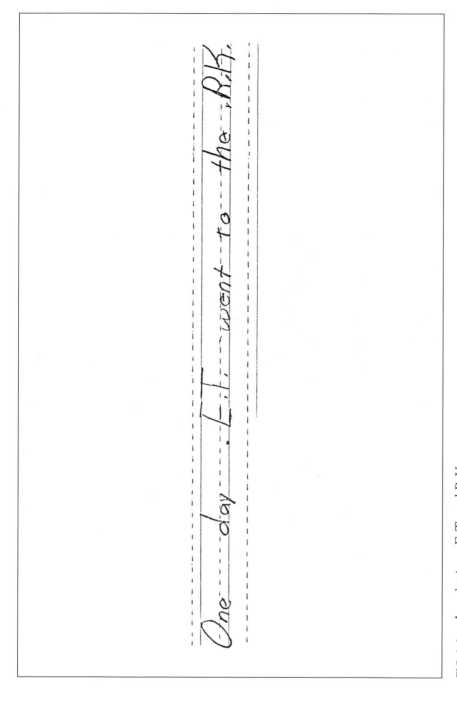

FIG 6-3 *Anna's piece: E.T. and R.K.*

FIG 6-4 *Barbara's piece: "The Island Family"*

name strategy. It's particularly amusing because the standard, adult spelling of VCR is a letter-name spelling.

A major early developmental task for young spellers is to realize that normally all the phonemes of a word are represented, that we use the letter *v*, for instance, to signify just /v/, not /vē/ (since written English is alphabetic, not syllabic). Most children grasp this principle by sometime in first grade. Barbara has actually moved beyond this realization and is exploring different ways to spell long vowels, as we see not only in VEASYARE but in BROAK and THERE (*their*). Should a teacher step in and correct her spelling of VCR? I'd be inclined to give her a chance to discover it for herself, perhaps saying something like, "That's a great spelling of VCR; you have letters for all the sounds. Why don't you look for a VCR ad in the newspaper and see how close you got?" Once she did that, you could talk with her about how a few words are normally spelled as abbreviations, like *VCR* and *TV*. (She had, of course, probably already seen *TV* in print.)

Leaving Out n's

Cathryn's note to me (Figure 6–5) has five *n*'s in it but is also missing two, in THAEKE (*thank*) and in the suffix of INVIEDG (*inviting*). Why these two? As we saw in Chapter 1, when a nasal sound comes before another consonant, children don't always represent it in their spelling, since it's not pronounced as strongly; this is what's going on with *thank*. Children eventually figure out that these *n*'s should be represented, and indeed we see that in Cathryn's spellings of *Sand* (a shortened version of my name) and *and*.

Cathryn's spelling of *inviting* may seem like the same phenomenon, but let's not be too hasty. Remember that what we usually spell with *ng* is actually a single phoneme, (/ŋ/), that's phonetically close to /g/, but is a nasal consonant rather than a voiced stop. So Cathryn is representing one phoneme with the letter for a related one rather than omitting a sound. Both of these omissions of *n* are normal; neither one needs any particular instructional support. Representing nasal sounds before consonants gets more consistent with more exposure to words in print, while spelling a phonetically similar sound is a common, general pattern of invented spelling that also diminishes

FIG 6–5   *Cathryn's piece: "Dir, Sand"*

greatly as spelling gets less phonetic. (Also, of course, children come to remember the *-ing* suffix from their experience with reading.) Read (1975) suggests that any instruction about nasals before consonants should at least recognize what's going on (I'd eliminate Read's *proba-blys*; I think he's being overly tentative—but he *is* writing in 1975):

> When children spell PUP (or POP, or whatever) for *pump*, there is probably nothing wrong with their hearing; they simply have no special symbol for the nasalized vowel that is the largest difference between *pump* and *pup*. . . . Accordingly, we suggest that teachers should *not* say something like, "No, what you wrote was HUT; what I said was *hunt*. Listen—Hunnnnt!" . . . The child probably knows what the teacher said, so these instructions are probably not useful. It would seem better to compare words like *Ben* and *bent*, and to point out that we regard them as containing the same sound. (116)

Problems with Digraphs

Poor Adrienne! She completely bombed out on her first-grade spelling test on *sh* words (Figure 6–6); she didn't get a single one of the six words right. (As her teacher commented, "Oops!") Normally Adrienne got 100 percent on her spelling tests, but that week she hadn't studied, so her spellings were a reflection of her preexisting level of spelling development. Unfortunately, if her teacher had done any instruction about the *sh* digraph, that didn't sink in either; none of Adrienne's spellings started with *sh*. They all started with *s*, the symbol for a closely related phoneme (they're both unvoiced frica-tives that occur close to each other at the roof of the mouth), and two of her spellings had *h*'s, but at the end of the word.

Is there something about digraphs that makes them harder to spell? Yes; you can hear an /s/ in the name of the letter *s* (/ɛs/), but no letter name contains the *sh* sound (/š/). It's therefore not surprising that Read (1975) discovered that the young children he studied spelled /s/ with *s* 87 percent of the time, but that they used *sh* for /š/ only 53 percent of the time.

Would Adrienne have been better off if she'd memorized these *sh* words for her spelling test? This raises two further questions: First, would she have remembered the correct spellings and transferred

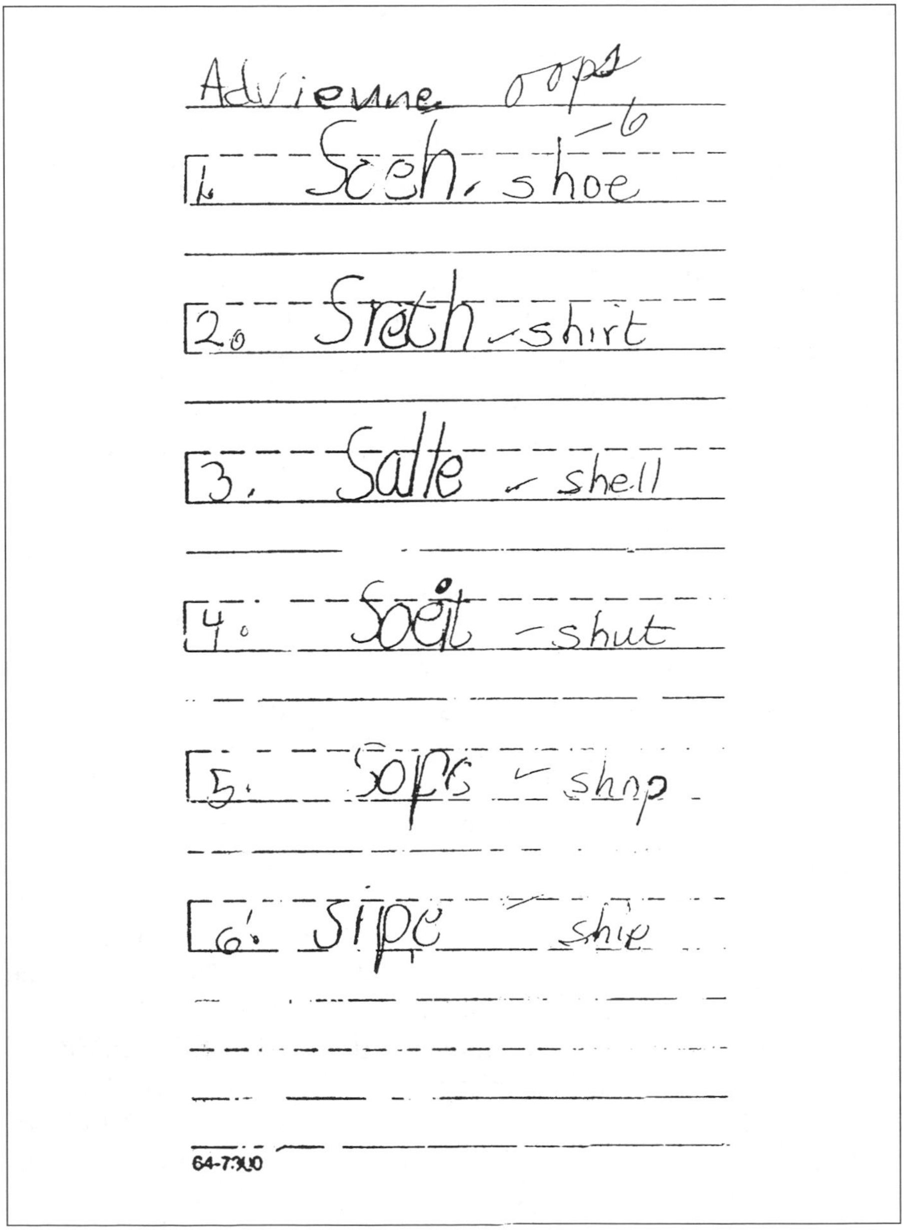

Adrienne oops
-6
1. Sceh. shoe

2. Sreth - shirt

3. Satte - shell

4. Soet - shut

5. Sops - shop

6. Sipe - shoe

64-7:300

FIG 6–6   *Adrienne's first test: "Soeh"*

them to her writing given that her invented spellings were so far off from the standard ones? I question the wisdom of a child's memorizing words when she can't even spell the first phoneme in them conventionally on her own. Second, would we be making her spend time memorizing something that she'd probably pick up on her own anyway?

Fortunately, we have evidence to answer this question, Adrienne's perfect spelling of the same words about a year and a half later (Figure 6–7). If we hadn't seen her earlier test, we might think that she knew how to spell these words in third grade because she'd learned them for her first-grade test, but we know she hadn't! She acquired them, rather, through her natural development as a reader and writer; by third grade she had, presumably, both the phonics knowledge to produce a regularly spelled word like *shop* and the individual word knowledge to spell *shoe*. What value could there have been in spending some of her valuable first-grade time memorizing these words? In general, one of the important things our kidwatching and knowledge about normal development does is let us resist feeling that we have to teach everything; it lets us trust that learners will pick up a great deal on their own.

Spelling the Way You Talk

Bill's piece (Figure 6–8) says, "I don't know what I will write about today. I thought and thought and I still couldn't. Never mind. Here I am thinking." (Notice the brainwave coming out of his head!) Most of his spellings are pretty typical except for the *f*'s at the beginning of *thought* and *thinking*. He's a native speaker of English with, as far as I know, normal language. Yet geography explains these spellings. He's from Australia, and Australia has a version of English that's similar to the London working-class Cockney dialect (remember that Australia was originally settled by prisoners). In this dialect, unvoiced *th* (/θ/) sometimes becomes /f/ and voiced *th* (/ð/) becomes /v/ (Horvath 1985). Just like all young children, then, Bill is spelling the way he speaks; to him *thought* and *fought* are homophones to some extent and he'll have to learn to spell them differently, just like *know* and *no*.

Larry's picture caption about Diego Rivera (Figure 6–9), which I

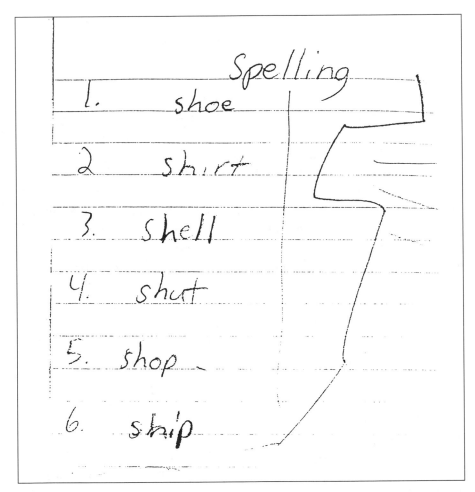

FIG 6–7   *Adrienne's second test: "Shoe"*

downloaded from his kindergarten classroom's homepage on the Internet, is an example of a different kind of spelling that represents speech. When Larry writes HEMAKT•PIKCHRS•, he's not saying "He made pictures" but rather "He maked pictures." Young children's word forms such as past tenses and possessives are sometimes different from those of adults, and a spelling such as BRANG or HISSELF isn't a "misspelling" of *brought* or *himself* but an accurate rendition of what the child is saying. As their speech matures, children's written versions of these words will reflect it (although some child language

96

FIG 6–8   *Bill's piece: "I dot no wot"*

97

FIG 6–9   *Larry's piece: "Diego Rivera"*

forms have started to enter adult speech; I've not only heard adults say *funner* but seen it in ads for the Oregon state lottery).

Higher-Level Features in Spelling

As children mature as spellers, we can start looking for patterns of what they still invent even as their spelling gets increasingly sophisticated in both quantity (number of words spelled right) and quality (types of invented spelling).

Word Boundaries in Older Children

As we explored when looking at Nat's captions for his caterpillar and butterfly drawing, spacing between words develops pretty early in children's writing. But Ken's gory werewolf story (Figure 6–10) has a few words that are spaced incorrectly: *once upon a time* is ONES A

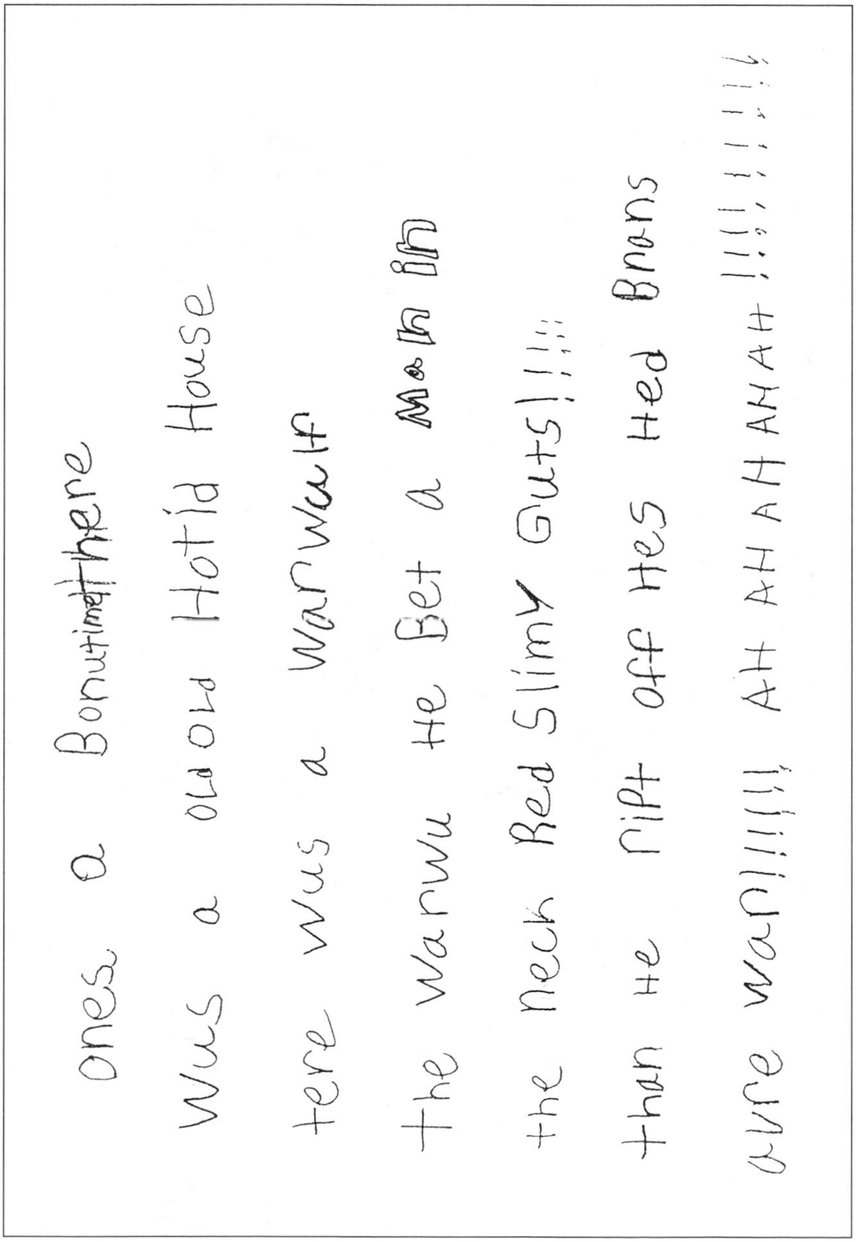

Ones a Bonutimethere

Wus a old old Hot'd House

tere Wus a WarWulf

The WarWu He Bet a Moln Bln

the Neck Red Slimy Guts!!!!!

than He ript off Hes Hed Bnons

aure wan!!!!!!; AH AH AH AH AH !!!!!!!!!!!;

FIG 6–10   *Ken's piece: "Ones a bonutime"*

99

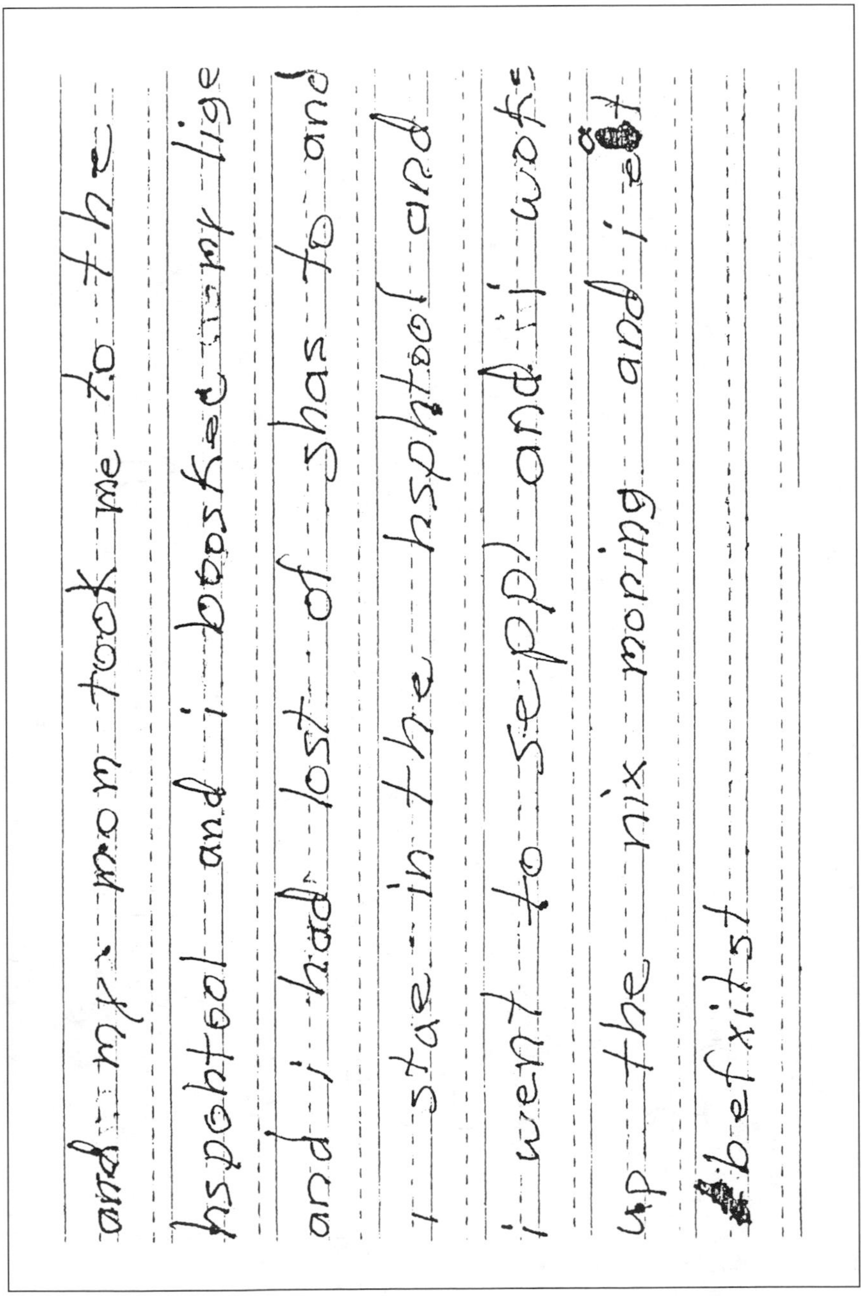

and my mom took me to the hspohtool and i botosked for lige and i had lost of shas to and stae in the hsphtool and i went to sepp and i wof up the nix moring and i et befxitst

FIG 6–11   Elaine's piece: "And my mom"

BONUTIME and *everywhere* is AVRE WAR.

Not surprisingly, when children who are for the most part spacing accurately between words have lapses, it involves a few special cases. Literate adults conceptualize the familiar phrase *once upon a time* as four separate words that retain their individual meanings, but for young children who have perhaps heard fairy tales aloud more often than they've read them themselves, the phrase works as a unit that signals the beginning of a story of a particular genre. They therefore sometimes write it all run together or, as in Ken's case, phrase it parallel to *once a night: once a bonutime*. Compound words like *everywhere*, perhaps particularly when they begin with a common adjective, tend to get separated, since it's hard to know the difference between a word like *everyone* and a two-word phrase like *every boy* unless you've seen them in print (let alone the difference between "*everyone* [was there]" and "*every one* [of them was there]." Such spacing problems are rare, however; in my dissertation study of third- and fourth-grade spelling, I found that six children used two words for one (e.g., BASE BALL and OUT SIDE) at a rate of only about once every two hundred words and one word for two (like RODEO-QUEEN and WAKEUP) only about once in every six hundred words.

Ken's piece reveals a lot about his spelling. We see that although he's spelled more words right than not, his invented spelling is still pretty phonetic; for instance, he uses the most common spelling of the short vowels in WUS, HOTID, and HED because he doesn't know the less regular conventional spelling. HOTID and RIPT also tell us that Ken hasn't generalized the spelling of the past-tense suffix but is still spelling it phonetically. When we look at the words Ken got right, we see that many of them are pretty easy because they're spelled regularly (*old*, *man*, *red*, and *guts*). Although Ken has spelled about two thirds of the words in his story accurately, we shouldn't let this camouflage the relative unsophistication of his knowledge about spelling.

Unusual Spellings

A section of Elaine's writing (Figure 6–11), excerpted from a longer piece, reads, "and my mom took me to the hospital and I broke my leg and I had lots of shots too and I stayed in the hospital and I went to sleep and I woke up the next morning and I ate breakfast."

Some of Elaine's spellings are fairly typical of what we see in many children: the final e rather than y in STAE, EAT for *ate*, the omission of the r in MONING. But several of her spellings are very unusual: HSPOHTOOL (hospital), BOOSKEC (broke), SEPPL (sleep), and BEFXITST (breakfast; in another piece she spelled it DILFTSCT). I've written about Elaine before (Wilde 1989a, 1992) because she's such a good example of how children's knowledge can sometimes be misunderstood.

When I've shared Elaine's writing samples with teachers, they often ask whether she is dyslexic, hearing impaired, speech impaired, an ESL student, developmentally disabled, learning disabled—you name the label. The assumption is that because her spelling is so unusual, there must be something wrong. My rule of thumb is that when we see something unusual, which some of her spelling indeed is, it's a signal to probe further. Having worked extensively with Elaine over a two-year period, I know that she spelled like this when she wanted to get her ideas out quickly, since she wasn't a good enough speller to do a "good" invented spelling quickly, particularly for longer words. It was a strategy choice, nothing more.

What should teachers do when they see a child spelling like this? The first step is to intensify the kidwatching—sit down with her as she writes, observing and asking how she came up with her unusual spelling. In Elaine's case, it was an appropriate strategy choice, and she needed to continue reading and otherwise grow in literacy before her spelling would get much better. What a disservice it would have been to try to "remediate" her spelling too soon.

Kidwatching with your students may of course have different results—you may discover, for instance, that they don't indeed know much about letter-sound relationships yet (unlike Elaine, who could produce better invented spelling if she took more time). But understanding the spelling from the child's perspective is the best way to start understanding how to work with her.

On a lighter note, Adrienne also used some unusual spelling in her birthday card to me (Figure 6–12). Her spelling of *Happy Birthday*

FIG 6–12 *Adrienne's birthday card*

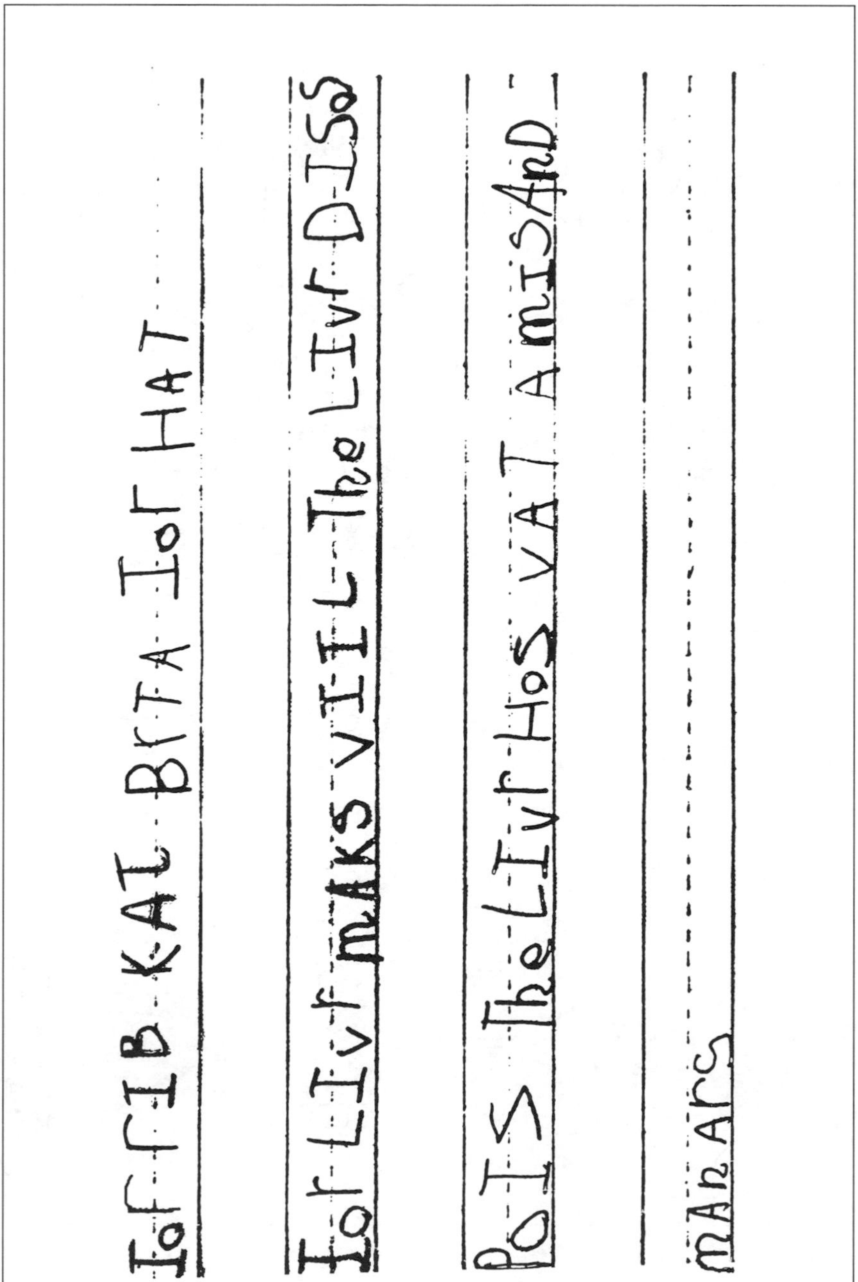

Iof fiB KAL BrtA Iof HAT

Iof Livf mAks ViiL The Livf DISS

PoIS The Livf HoS VAT A miSAnD

mARArS

FIG 6–13 *Jason's piece: "Your rib cage"*

was unusual on purpose; she knows that I do research on spelling and enjoy invented spelling. (In her words, "Ha! Ha! Ha!") What makes this card even funnier is that her invented spelling of *spelling* was unintentional. By the way, did you notice that Adrienne and Cathryn (Figure 6–5) both wrote "Dear, Sandra" in their salutations? When more than one child does the same thing in written language, there's usually a general principle behind it. I believe that in both cases they were overgeneralizing the rule for punctuation in the closing of a letter (as in "Love, Cathryn") and put a comma before the name in the salutation as well.

Substituting One Sound for Another

We saw in Chapter 1 how Jason (see Figure 6–13) used phonetically related sounds to represent the initial phonemes of *protects* and *bile*. When a child makes substitutions like this, is it a sign of problems with a particular sound? Let's look at his piece again for patterns in how he spells the related sounds /b/, /p/, and /v/. First, here's how the sounds are related (/f/ is included in this table although Jason didn't use it in this piece):

	Voiced	Unvoiced
Bilabial stop	/b/	/p/
Labiodental fricative	/v/	/f/

Now let's look at how Jason spells the three sounds:

/b/	b: RIB v: VIIL (bile)
/p/	b: BRTA (protects) p: POIS (poison)
/v/	v: LIVR, VATAMIS (vitamins)

Although he did substitute related phonemes, he certainly didn't do so consistently. Also, his substitutions involved a change either in voicing (*b* for /p/) or in manner of articulation (a fricative for a stop, along with a slight change of place of articulation, in VIIL); he never substituted a sound that occurred in a completely different place in the mouth. My experience with Jason told me that much of his invented spelling was the result of overarticulation as he painstakingly sounded out words. (Writing was still quite slow for him, and he'd been classified as learning disabled—but also as gifted.)

It's also interesting to see how close some of his spellings are to phonetic representations:

Word	Jason's	Phonetic spelling
your	IOR	/ɪɔr/ (if we view it as starting with a glide rather than a consonant)
poison	POIZ	/pɔizən/
bile	VIIL	/bɪɪl/ (if we view it as broken into two accented syllables)

What may be most important about Jason's spelling in this piece is that, although it may be somewhat immature for late second grade, it's not at all random but quite logical. As always, an awareness of children's strengths can help us build on what they already know—in this case perhaps by helping him speed up a little what he's already doing reasonably well: making connections between sounds and the letters that represent them.

Problems in Spelling a Particular Sound

It's useful to look at a child's writing for a consistent pattern of sounds involved in his or her invented spelling. When we look at Chad's piece (Figure 6–14), we can group his invented spelling according to the part of the word he "got wrong"; let's look at two examples:

Phoneme	Got it wrong	Got it right
/w/	WHANTED	was, when
/ʌ/	BECUSE, OUTHER	was, from

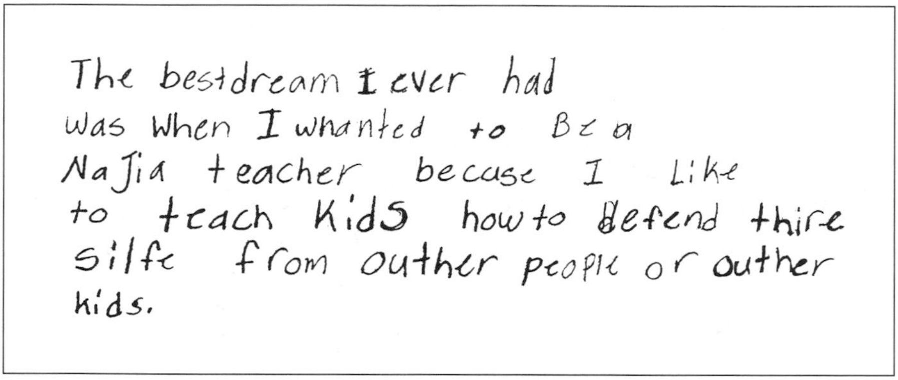

The best dream I ever had
was when I whanted to Be a
NaJia teacher becuse I Like
to teach Kids how to defend thire
silfe from outher peoplc or outher
kids.

FIG 6–14   *Chad's piece: "The best dream I ever had"*

Knowing that /w/ (in most versions of American English) has both *w* and *wh* as common spellings and that short *u* (/ʌ/) can be spelled in other ways than *u*, particularly in common words, makes Chad's spelling very understandable. As we saw in Chapter 1, children almost always need to sort out *w* and *wh* words without a phonetic way to tell them apart; it's a matter of knowing which one applies to a particular word, and Chad had that knowledge for two out of three of the /w/ words in his piece.

Chad used a *u* in one invented spelling of the short *u* sound, while in the other one he used *ou*, which is how /ʌ/ is spelled in words like *cousin* and *double*. He got the sound right in *was* and *from*, even though these spellings are less common.

It would therefore be a real mistake to say that he had "problems" with either of these phonemes; rather, he understood at a developing level the different ways they're spelled, and was gradually learning exactly how they're spelled in particular words.

Phonetic and Visual Spellings as Kids Get Older
Often as children learn to spell better, their spelling gets more "visual" in the sense that they show a lot of knowledge of having seen that specific word in print. For instance, they might have all the right letters but in the wrong order (like Adrienne's SEPLLING) or be correct except for the spelling of the vowel (like Chad's OUTHER).

107

Some day I would like to goyne
the circus. Do you know what
I want to be? I want to be a
athropist lady and my soot
would be people with dimends

FIG 6–15   *Cheri's piece: "Some day I would like to goyne"*

But sometimes we see children who seem to be spelling a number of words very phonetically still, as in third-grade Cheri's piece (Figure 6–15), which reads, "Someday I would like to join the circus. Do you know what I want to be? I want to be a trapeze lady and my suit would be purple with diamonds." What makes this piece especially interesting is that out of thirty-one words, only six use invented spelling and five of those (the exception is her spelling of *someday* as two words) are spelled quite phonetically; that is, they're wrong because she made an inappropriate but reasonable choice in spelling one or more sounds:

join	GOYNE
trapeze	CHRAPIES
suit	SOOT
purple	PERPLE
diamonds	DIMENDS

Cheri's phonetic spellings are perfectly good ones. All the phonemes are represented, the double *o* in SOOT is analogous to *boot*, and the only somewhat immature features (which aren't bad, just less common at her age) are using *g* to represent /j/ before *o* and using *ch* to represent the affricated /t/ before *r* of *trapeze*. The latter may result from an idiosyncracy in her speech; I have another piece where she wrote about finding a CHEANCHILA on her bed. (If you know anything about southern Arizona, where she lives, it's easy to figure out that she found not a chinchilla but a tarantula!)

Older writers' spelling that is more visual than phonetic may look better, but in both cases the issue is how children can get better at getting all of the words right for a final draft, which comes down to learning to be a good proofreader of your own writing.

Specific Spelling Features in Older Writers

Just as younger writers have the task of figuring out how to represent each sound of English in their spelling, older writers explore finer

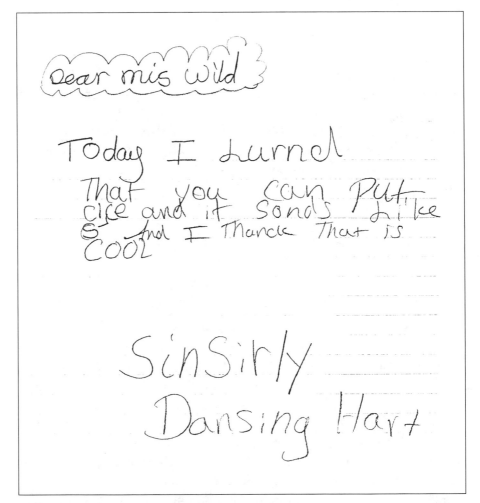

FIG 6–16   *Randy's letter: "Dear Mis Wild"*

nuances such as a particular sound represented by more than one letter, double letters, and the spelling of suffixes and homophones.

Spelling /s/ and /k/

In some ways the letter *c* is unnecessary in written English (except in
ch), since we could use *s* or *k* to represent the sounds it spells. The ad-
vantage that *c* gives us, however, is that it allows the related mean-

ings of words to be apparent even when the sound changes; without *c*, *critic* and *criticize* would be replaced by *kritik* and *kritisize*. The disadvantage, of course, is that it's a little harder to learn to spell these sounds.

When I conducted a class minilesson that included the information that *c* before *e* or *i* makes an /s/ sound, Randy wrote me a letter about what she'd learned (Figure 6–16) that also revealed that her spelling of /s/ and /k/ was still developing. She wrote, "Dear Miss [or Ms.?] Wilde, Today I learned that you can put ci, ce and it sounds like s. And I think that is cool. Sincerely, Dancing Heart [her nickname]." Yet despite what she said in the letter, every time she represented /s/, she used a single letter *s*. This worked some of the time, but not in MIS (if it meant *Miss*), the second /s/ of SINSIRLY, or DANSING. Clearly, explicit knowledge of a spelling pattern doesn't always transfer to the spelling of particular words, which will improve as a student's knowledge of particular words grows. (And of course, it isn't always possible to apply knowledge of spelling patterns accurately: why is there only one *c* in *sincerely* when *cincerely* would also work?) Interestingly, Randy is more flexible in her spelling of /k/, using *c* appropriately in *can* and *cool* and *k* in *like*, and she also knows the *ck* spelling, even though she overgeneralizes it and uses it in THANCK (*think*). Again, the correct spelling is probably because she already knows the word.

Double Consonants

Here's Adrienne again (Figure 6–17), this time writing to skater Nancy Kerrigan (whose disgraced rival Tonya Harding is from Adrienne's hometown). Not only does Adrienne use double consonants everywhere they're needed (in four words), she also includes them in CHERRING and HARDDING.

Knowing when to use double consonants isn't easy; for instance, looking at Adrienne's accurate ones, *biggest* follows the rule for doubling before suffixes and the double consonant in *happened* is needed to show the vowel is short, but what about *Kerrigan* and *sorry*? And why isn't the *n* in *happened* doubled before the suffix? It's not at all surprising that children often either fail to double consonants or

111

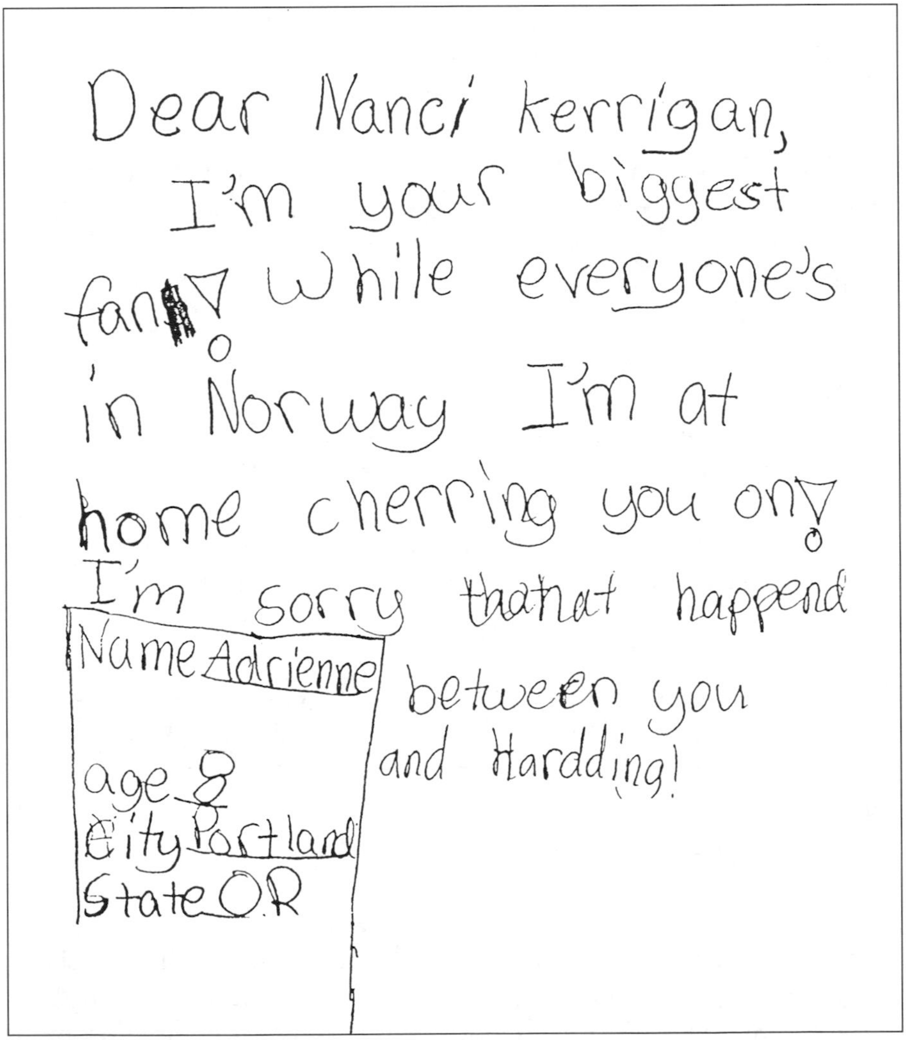

Dear Nanci kerrigan,
I'm your biggest
fansy While everyone's
in Norway I'm at
home cherring you ony
I'm sorry thathat happend
between you
and Hardding!

Name Adrienne
age 8
City Portland
State O.R

FIG 6–17 *Adrienne's letter to Nancy Kerrigan*

overuse them. (This is also a common invented spelling patern in the writing of adults, which suggests that it's a fairly difficult feature to grasp.)

Interestingly, Adrienne's two overgeneralizations of double consonants occur in words where they seem reasonable; she didn't double the consonants in words with long vowels like *home* or GRATE (*great*). Perhaps her tendency to over- rather than undergeneralize double consonants comes from her name; both her first and her last names have phonetically unnecessary double consonants.

Suffixes

Although Mark is a younger writer, I've used his piece (Figure 6–18) to illustrate suffixes because he uses three different ones in a short piece and also because his words ("I learned to sit quietly. I learned to spell better") are so comically at odds with his spelling!

Mark's spelling of the -ed, -ly, and -er suffixes are purely phonetic (and he omits the suffix entirely the second time he writes *learned*). Children's ability to spell suffixes develops through roughly three stages: spelling the suffix phonetically, spelling the suffix as a consistent morpheme (meaning unit), and applying rules for changing root words before suffixes. The way we work with children on suffixes should respond to where they are in their development.

We've seen other examples of phonetic spelling of the -ing suffix in Nat's DACEN (*drinking*) and Cathyrn's INVIEDG (*inviting*), and phonetic spellings of the past tense in Larry's MAKT (*maked*), Ken's HOTID (*haunted*) and RIPT, and Randy's LURND.

The past-tense suffix is especially likely to be spelled phonetically because it has three different pronunciations: /t/ as in *ripped*, /d/ as in *learned*, and /əd/ as in *haunted*. Even though the -s suffix (in plurals and verbs) also has three pronunciations, children tend to figure out quite early that it's consistently spelled s, perhaps because plurals are so common. None of the writing samples we've looked at used z instead of s for a plural suffix.

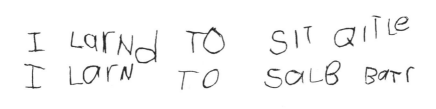

FIG 6–18   *Mark's piece: "I larned to sit qitle"*

When children who are otherwise not beginners spell suffixes phonetically, it might make sense to conduct a minilesson to help them realize that suffixes are spelled abstractly. (The past-tense suffix is the one they most often misspell and is therefore the one most useful to teach.) You could do this by writing some present-tense verbs on the board, changing them to past tense with the children's help, and then asking them what they notice. (Pick words whose root doesn't change before the suffix to keep things simple, but be sure to include words that reflect all three pronunciations of the suffix.) See Wilde 1992, p. 78, for another example of a past tense minilesson.

Barbara's ROBER (Figure 6–4) reveals that she has learned to spell a suffix but doesn't yet know the rule for doubling a final consonant before adding the suffix, while Adrienne's *biggest* shows that she knows the rule. Barbara would be ready for a minilesson on changes to root words, while Mike is not yet ready and Adrienne wouldn't need one. This minilesson would take a similar form to the previous one: putting words and their inflected forms on the board and asking students what they notice. (Refer to Chapter 3, p. 36, to review the rules for changes before suffixes.)

Homophones

Virtually every spelling textbook contains a lesson on homophones at some point during the year. Pairs of words that presumably are easily confused are presented together, used in exercises, and substituted for each other in proofreading activities. It's my (as yet unproven) hunch that focusing on these words may make children *more* likely to confuse them. I'm indebted to Frank Smith (1982) for the idea that often we spell words wrong not because we can't remember the right spelling but because we can't forget the wrong one. (I only began to confuse *there* and *their* after I became a teacher and started seeing them substituted for each other in children's writing.)

Perhaps we should avoid formal teaching from a list of homophones, since it may encourage children to set up connections between pairs of words that they'd then be more likely to confuse with each other. Why not instead see what problems with homophones persist after children are spelling a number of common words consistently, and then work specifically on those?

Elaine's piece (Figure 6–19) has two homophone substitutions, ARE for *our* and RODE for *road*. (The excerpt reads, "Then the sun was up. And it was brighting [sic] in our eyes. Then we couldn't see and we almost went off the road.") Elaine's class had been studying homophones that week, which clearly didn't prevent them in her writing. Neither of the homophone pairs involved in these substitutions would be likely to turn up in a textbook, since such lessons usually include root words and not inflected (e.g., past-tense) forms like *rode*, and because *are* and *our* aren't homophones in every dialect of English (although *our*, in its more "proper" pronunciation, is sometimes presented as a homophone of *hour*).

How are homophone substitutions best dealt with? Probably as part of general proofreading, and knowing that they're hard to catch because the speller has written a real word that's an alternative representation of the same sequence of sounds. Also, homophones can be discussed in relation to similar words rather than to each other. A child who gets *there* wrong can be shown that it's *here* plus a *t*; if she misses *their*, she can be helped to see its similarity to *they*. If it's any consolation, homophone substitutions turn up all the time in the writing of adults. I recently came across (in a book, which presumably went through several levels of proofreading) a reference to the "grizzly" (i.e., *grisly*) O. J. Simpson murders.

We might assume that homophone substitutions are a big problem in spelling since they stand out strongly when we read a piece, but in my doctoral study (Wilde 1986/1987), I found that third and fourth graders, when writing words that have homophones, substituted a homophone only 5.1 percent of the time. (They had another invented spelling for these words 5.7 percent of the time.) Most of the homophone substitutions involved five spellings: TO for too, THERE for *their*, ARE for *our*, WOOD for *would*, and HOLE for *whole*. Another study (Fisher & Studier 1977) found that homophone substitutions accounted for 7 percent of intermediate-grade children's invented spellings, with the pairs *there/their*, *too/to*, and *know/no* accounting for half of these. Perhaps once children realize

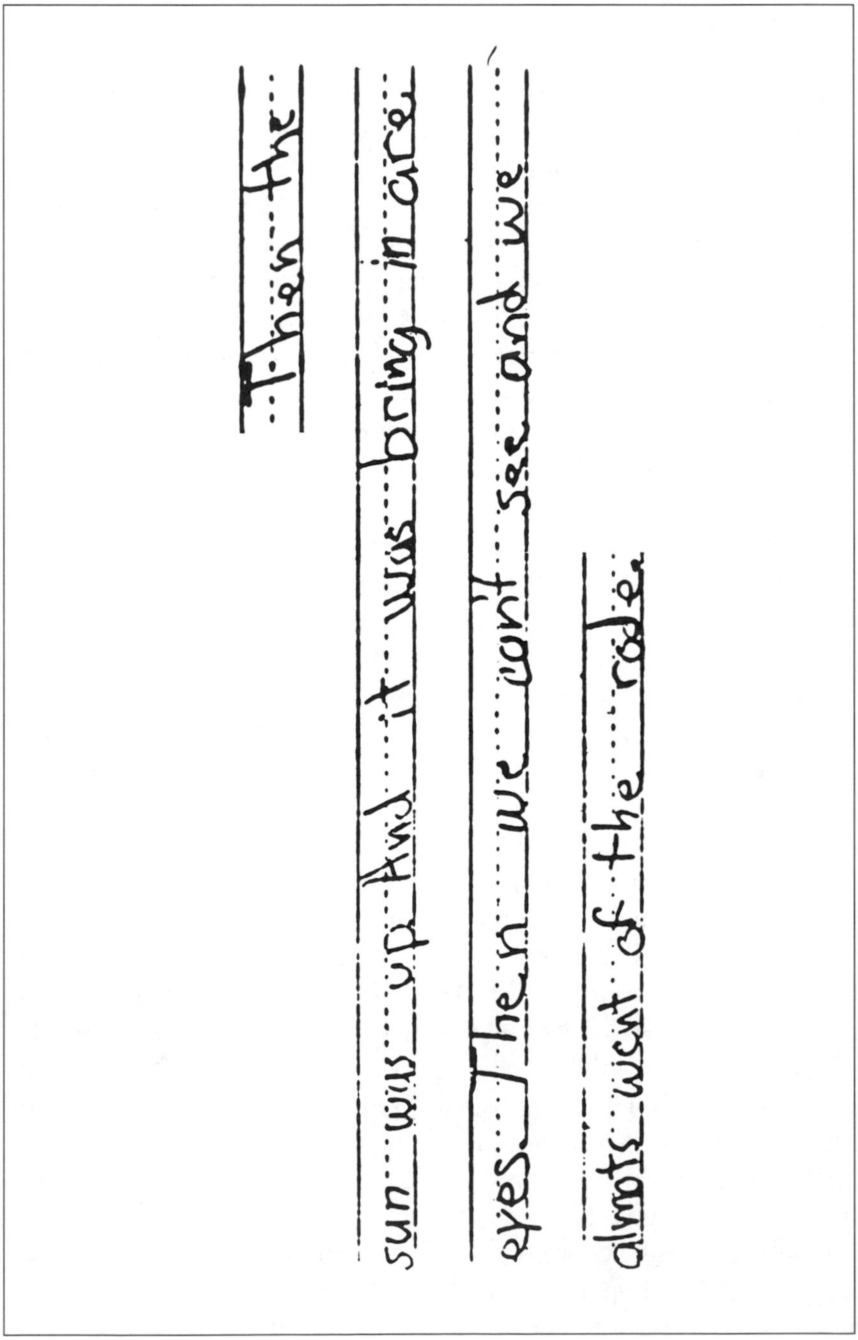

FIG 6–19 *Elaine's piece: "Then the sun was up"*

that the same sequence of sounds is sometimes spelled in more than one way, the most valuable strategy is to become aware of the ones they are most likely to confuse, and then to watch for those specifically when proofreading.

Fine-Tuning

As children become increasingly mature spellers, we can often identify one or two features of invented spelling that still remain and to which we might want to devote some extra attention. These often involve patterns or strategies that apply broadly across many words.

Easy Words Spelled Wrong

Sometimes children's spelling drives us crazy because they seem to get some very easy words wrong. We can look at Gordon's piece (Figure 6–20) and see that he spelled *parrot* and *night* correctly, and appreciate that he tried to spell *incredible* even though he came up with INGRRDBOLL (note the g substituted for the phonetically related /k/).

But why did he do so well on these harder words, yet get *there*, *two*, and *would* wrong? And I've frequently heard teachers complain that kids are always writing THAY for *they*, GRIL for *girl*, and so on. What's going on with these easy words?

I believe that we're misperceiving the situation, that children spell common, easy, frequently used words with an extremely high degree of accuracy. In my doctoral research, the six children I studied spelled the thirty-seven words they used most often, which made up 50 percent of their running text, correctly 98 percent of the time.

Let's look at some of the bugaboos that teachers often mention as problems: my six research subjects had 248 correct spellings of *went* and 19 invented ones (11 of them WANT, none of them WHENT); 163 correct spellings of *they* and 17 invented ones (11 of them THAY); 110 correct spellings of *said* and 39 invented ones (9 of them SIAD); 91 correct spellings of *there* and 17 invented ones (Gordon, in Figure 6–20, had the only instance of THEIR for *there*).

Such spellings can be frustrating, particularly in older children,

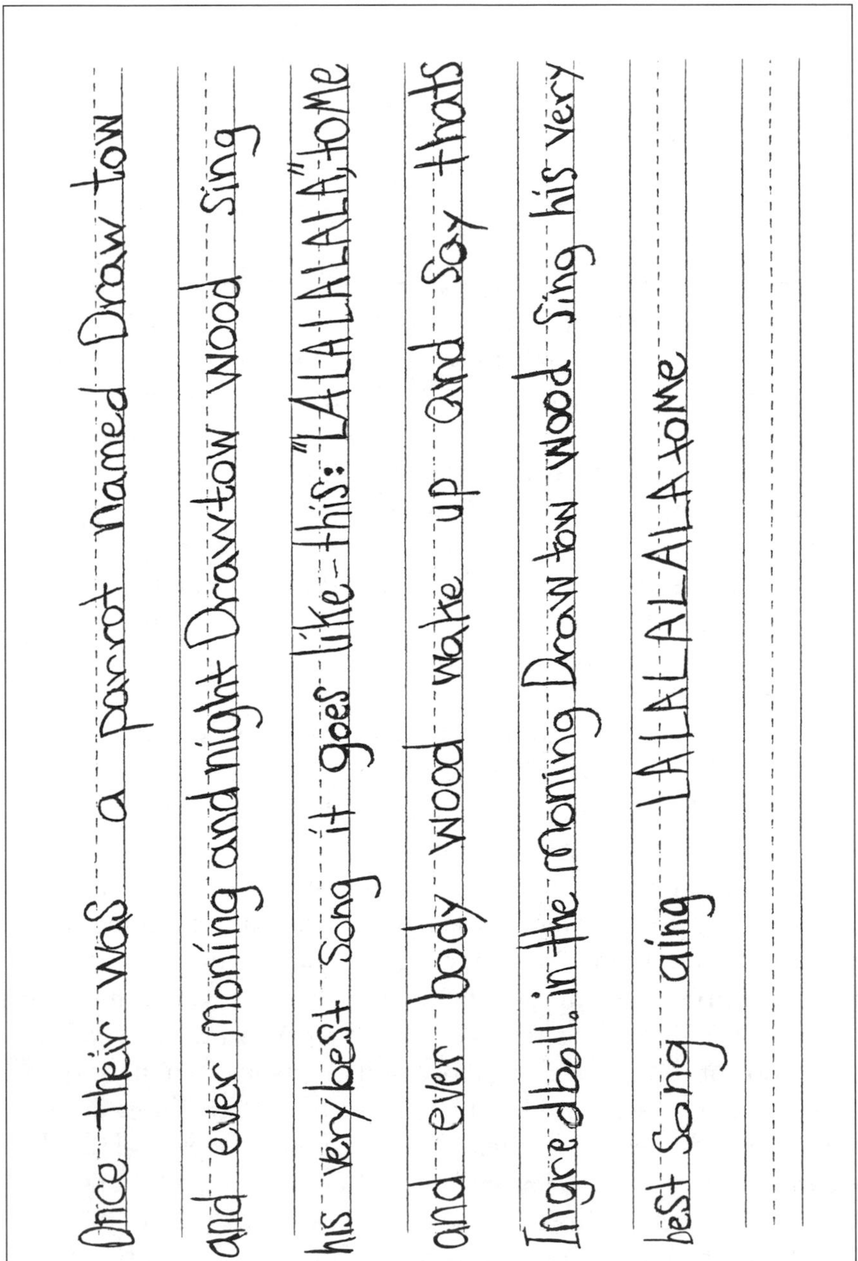

Once their was a parrot Named Draw tow
and ever moning and night Drawtow Wood Sing
his very best Song it goes like this: "LALALALALA tome"
and ever body Wood wake up and say thats
Ingredabll in the moning Draw tow Wood sing his very
best Song aing LALALALALA tome

FIG 6–20   Gordon's piece: "Once their was a parrot"

but it's probably not a very big problem very much of the time. Words that are frequently encountered simply aren't spelled wrong very often, while the less common words for which children invent spellings don't occur as often in overall text. Teachers who spend a lot of time working on lists of frequently used words with children may be putting energy into teaching them what they already know (or, if done at a younger age, teaching them what they'd pick up on their own).

Clearly, children should be helped to do better on the relatively easy words they miss, and they can be taught to monitor their own writing to discover what these words are. Although one might assume from looking at Gordon's piece that he was being "careless" about his spelling, field notes taken as he wrote it reveal that he was instead very focused on spelling. He copied the spelling of *parrot* from the researcher's notes (she had written that he'd asked, "How do you spell *parrot*?"); his invented spelling of *two* came from a miscopying: he'd gotten the parrot's name (*Draw Two*) from a card in the board game *Sorry*. At one point he asked the researcher if *there* was spelled right, and after writing THATS, he said, "That's how you spell *that's*, huh?" in both cases showing that he was interested in spelling words correctly. We can sometimes be too quick to assume that children don't care about or pay attention to spelling as they write, when in fact they may be grappling with it quite assiduously given the limitations of their knowledge and everything else that a writer needs to focus on.

Missing Letters

As spelling becomes more sophisticated, we increasingly see invented spelling that is off by a single letter, often a missing one—silent letters, vowels preceding *r* (and sometimes vowels preceding *m*, *n*, or *l*), phonetic spelling of suffixes, consonant clusters, and long words.

Peter's birthday note to his mom (Figure 6–21) has three words that are missing letters, BRTHDAY, NO, and WA, and two of these involve silent letters. It's also easy to understand the omitted vowel in *birthday*, since an /r/ tends to "swallow up" the preceding vowel. (Peter's spelling of WROD for *word* is actually very similar, since the /r/ seems to occur right after the /w/, but in this case he probably also

Happy Brthday, I
dont no if this is
The Kite un to
sPell The wrad
Brthday Love Peter

FIG 6–21   *Peter's birthday note*

knew that the word had an *o* in it so put it in next. Therefore his spelling of *word* had all the right letters but in the wrong order, a type of high-level invented spelling.)

Leaving out letters is partly developmental (familiarity with silent letters, spelling *-ed* consistently) and partly a proofreading issue, particularly when longer words are involved; sometimes children seem to run out of steam when coming up with a spelling for a longer word, and need to learn to recognize that it's incomplete when they reread their piece.

Sticking in Apostrophes

Trevor, a relatively unsophisticated third-grade speller—as we can see from both his spelling and his occasional letter reversals (Figure 6–22), wrote a piece that began, "Once I had a broken foot. It all started when I was over at my aunt's place. I went in the garage. I went to the vise." Trevor used apostrophes three times, appropriately in *aunt's* and inappropriately in WON'T (his original spelling of *once*) and WIN'T (*went*). When I asked him to try another spelling of *once*, he wrote WONT'S.

Although the use of apostrophes follows very specific rules, we shouldn't assume that it's through a precise application of the rules that children learn to use them. They're more likely to notice apostrophes in print and, perhaps with some explicit knowledge about them, start using them where they seem to make sense. If they've noticed that they occur in words that end with *s* and in short words that end with *t*, that may well be where they put them in their writing, regardless of whether they're appropriate. (Notice that Trevor's two overgeneralizations of apostrophes produce *n't* endings, as in *don't* and similar words.)

Apostrophes are conceptual (i.e., they replace a vowel in a contracted word), but children may well treat them more as visual features. Trevor might have benefited from a minilesson geared to help him discover the relationship between pairs like *do not* and *don't* (although given the general developmental lag in his writing and spelling, it might not be have been the highest priority for him at this point).

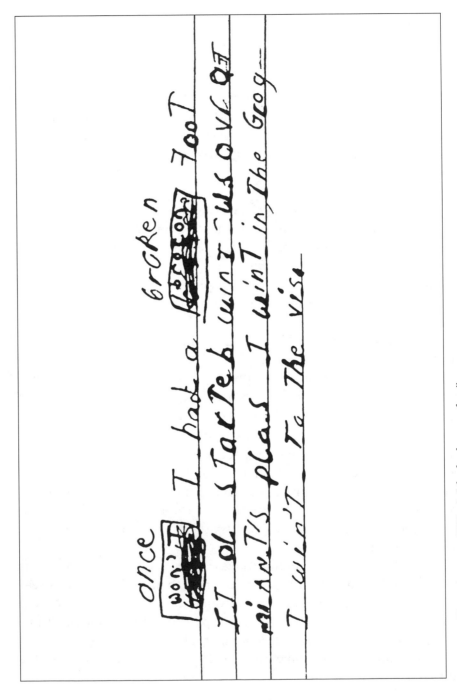

FIG 6–22   Trevor's piece: "Won't I had a brocon foot"

My Daughter's in Sixth Grade and Her Spelling's Still Terrible; What Should I Do?

Deirdre's mother called me for some advice; Deirdre's teacher wanted a conference about her spelling. Deirdre was heading for middle school the next year and the teacher was worried that the higher standards there would cause Deirdre a great deal of difficulty if her spelling didn't improve. I asked for a sample of Deirdre's writing and, after looking at it, agreed that it was problematic. Here's a section of it (with her invented spelling uppercased):

> The PROBLE [problem] ASK [asks] how MENY [many] miles DOS [does] light go in one year. WHE [when] I STARD [started] I NOW [knew] I was going T [to] have to do the problem in STEPES [steps]. FRIST [first] I had to know how fast light travels in one SCENT [second] so I asked my dad and he said 300,000 km. . . . I thought I had FISHED [finished] the problem and I was all DON [done], all I had to do was the WIGHTING [writing]. But I was ROWNG [wrong]. . . . To MACK [make] it into miles I had to DIVED [divide] 1.6 into 1 mile because THER [there] are 1.6 km. in 1 mile. Then I got my ANSTER [answer]! I had HEPL [help] from my dad's ROOMATE [roommate].

A quick analysis of Deirdre's spelling revealed that 85 percent of the words in the piece as a whole were spelled correctly, which certainly is not as good as we would expect from a child this age, particularly one with strong academic ambitions like Deirdre.

Looking at individual words, I noticed a few patterns: a number of them were missing just one letter (such as PROBLE, MENY) or had all the right letters but in the wrong order (ROWNG); other spellings had enough wrong with them that I wondered if they were quick guesses rather than good attempts to figure out the word (SCENT and FISHED); and she didn't always represent suffixes appropriately if at all (DOS for *does* and LOURND for *learned* later in the piece). I also knew from talking to her mother that Deirdre wasn't much of a reader.

I suggested working with Deirdre to see whether she could catch her invented spelling and edit it (the idea being to help her develop strategies and ownership for spelling in final-draft writing), and doing as much as possible to get her reading more. What a mistake it would have been to start drilling her on the common words that she missed a lot in her writing rather than working on these broader strategies.

As it turned out, Deirdre discovered Judy Blume's books the summer before middle school and finally turned into a voracious reader; her spelling improved dramatically and became only a minor problem.

A Final Word on Working with Invented Spelling

I hope the writing samples in this chapter have shown you the value of knowing how sounds and letters work together and also the value of looking at the larger picture of what kids are doing as they come up with a spelling for a word. They're indeed thinking, What letter goes with this sound? but they're also dealing with how written language is laid out on the page, what words look like, and multiple ways of representing the same sound, all of this in the context of trying to get their ideas out (which is rightfully the focus of their attention).

Perhaps the most important role we as teachers can play in this process is to respect and support students' growing knowledge and let our own knowledge of what they are doing—and a healthy dose of common sense—guide how we work with them.

SEVEN

Miscues: What They Tell Us About Children's Use of Phonics When They Read

As the previous chapter on invented spelling demonstrates, children's "errors" are rich sources of information about their knowledge of how written language works. In this chapter, let's examine a number of miscues produced by a single child and in so doing explore how phonics is used in reading.

First, a brief introduction to the concepts of miscue and miscue analysis. I'm using the term *miscue*, more comprehensive and less judgmental than the term *error*, as employed by Kenneth Goodman to refer to a reader's unexpected response to text. Miscues include substitutions (an American's reading *wait a minute* for *wait a moment*), omissions, insertions, and sometimes combinations of these in complex miscues. *Miscue analysis* (Goodman, Watson & Burke 1987) is a highly developed system of looking at miscues across a number of dimensions, including the graphophonic, in order to discover how readers make sense of text. Miscue analysis theory posits that the reading process is essentially the same when miscues occur and when they don't; in both cases, a search for meaning drives a process of sampling, predicting, confirming, and correcting, using graphophonic relationships and also the knowledge of language structure, meaning, and language use (*syntactics*, *semantics*, and *pragmatics*, respectively) that we bring to the reading process (K. Goodman 1996). Versions of miscue analysis can be used for highly elaborate research procedures or for everyday classroom use.

The great value of the perspective gained from miscue analysis—like the analysis of invented spelling, of which it is in many ways the precursor—is that it helps one see error not as bad but as informative. For instance, researchers in miscue analysis are unlikely to put much emphasis on comparing readers by looking at how many miscues they make, since readers are asked to read texts that evoke enough miscues to reveal the strategies they use when reading is difficult for them. This is extremely important: we're interested in looking not at *how well* readers do in a quantitative sense but in *what* they do qualitatively.

We're likely to discover in the process that some readers are better than others, but in ways that have to do with the strategies they use and that help us determine how to work with them more effectively. (It may also be useful to know at what level of difficulty a reader can process text comfortably, but tht's another question and one that miscue analysis isn't designed to answer.) Put another way, any reader will make miscues if given a text that is challenging for him or her (we want readers to make enough miscues to analyze, but not to read a text so difficult that it loses all meaning).

All miscues involve phonics in the sense that they're a deviation from what's "on the page" (that is, what we expect to hear). Some miscues appear to be a mispronunciation of the word, while others aren't even close—for instance, *the* may be substituted for *his*. Miscue analysis procedures therefore consider how close the miscue is graphically and phonetically. (All my descriptions of miscue analysis are based on Goodman, Watson & Burke 1987.) Many high-quality miscucs (i.e., those likely to be produced by good readers) aren't close on the graphophonic level but are grammatical and make sense in the text, so that miscue analysis also looks at syntactic and semantic acceptability.

This discussion highlights graphic similarity and also in many cases semantic acceptability and/or a change in meaning. Although much of this book deals with the sounds of English, and a full miscue analysis deals with both graphic and phonetic similarity, I want to keep it simple and focus on what seems the more informative of the two. Often graphic and phonetic similarity are comparable, as in reading *coat* for *cat*. But in a miscue like *hose* for *house*, the spelling similarity helps explain the miscue even though the two words end with different sounds. Thus graphic similarity illuminates the reader's use of phonics at least as much as phonetic similarity does, though I'll also mention phonetic similarity when it seems relevant.

Two simple examples of looking at miscues at the graphic and semantic levels: a miscue of *house* for *horse* in the sentence, "He rode away on a horse" is highly similar graphically, but the sentence doesn't work in terms of meaning. A miscue of *pony* would be just the opposite: graphically it's not at all like *horse*, but the meaning is virtually unchanged. *Pony* would be considered the better miscue because of the way it preserves meaning.

Two other dimensions I'll look at are self-correction—when and why does the reader correct her miscues, and what does this tell us about her?—and intentionality—does she appear aware that she's making a miscue or is it inadvertent (K. Goodman & Gollasch 1980)?

Obviously, word-perfect reading preserves the graphic, the phonic, and the semantic. But all readers make miscues (as anyone who's ever read aloud knows), and they give us insight into the meaning construction processes, including the use of phonics as one cueing system, that are also going on when no miscues occur.

Our subject, fifth grader Miranda, is not a very proficient reader. She is able to read and make sense of some texts (a picture book for example) but is not able to handle the novels and more sophisticated informational texts that are usual at this grade level. She writes somewhat fluently and uses a fair amount of generally sophisticated invented spelling.

The text I asked her to read was a picture book about seasonal changes in the Arctic called *Land of Dark, Land of Light: The Arctic National Wildlife Refuge* (Pandell 1993). Since I'm not able to reproduce the whole text with all of Miranda's miscues because of copyright restrictions, I won't provide an overall portrait of Miranda as a reader—but this is not my purpose here, anyway.

127

Rather, I'd like to show you the varied ways that a reader, confronted with text that challenges her, deals with the graphophonic system as she reads. Think of this as a collection of miscues that happen to come from one reader, rather than a miscue analysis of Miranda. (For those who aren't already familiar with miscue analysis, I strongly recommend consulting a source such as Y. Goodman, Watson & Burke [1987] to become familiar with the larger picture on which my discussion here is based.)

Miscues with Low Graphic Similarity

I'm starting with some miscues in which Miranda doesn't rely heavily on graphophonic information in the sense that her miscues involve no graphic similarity or only some (defined as about a third of the word).

Insertion, Semantically Acceptable

> Text: In the far north in winter. . .
> Miranda: In the far north in the winter. . .

When a reader inserts a word that doesn't exist in the text, there is of course no graphic similarity. (Technically, this miscue wouldn't normally be coded for graphic similarity, because only substitutions, not insertions, are coded for this dimension. I'm extrapolating a little from miscue procedure to focus on the larger issue of how readers use the graphic dimension.) Nevertheless, such miscues, which often, as in this case, appear to be inadvertent or unintentional, often are merely an alternative phrasing of the text. Would it be better to read the text without the miscue? Not necessarily. The time it takes to read a text word-perfectly isn't always worth it. This miscue (which probably represents Miranda's speech better than the phrasing in the text) is typical of those made by good readers.

Some Graphic Similarity, Minimal Meaning Change

> Text: A fox . . . in its warm winter coat.
> Miranda: A fox . . . in his warm winter coat.

I was amused by Miranda's reading of *his* for *its* in referring to a fox, since I've noticed how often people use a generic *he* with animals (unless it's obviously female, like a cow). When I played a tape of her reading back to Miranda, she was a little surprised at the miscue, and we talked about how the male pronoun is common with animals. This is an easy miscue to make, since both *his* and *its* are short possessive pronouns. It's also a good example of how phonics really has little to do with such miscues; common sense tells us that this miscue is not a mispronunciation of *its* but the result of rapid reading in which Miranda recognized that the word was a short function word but then made a reasonable prediction rather than looking more closely in order to get it exactly right. Again, it reflects the reader's speech and changes the meaning virtually not at all.

Some Graphic Similarity, Corrected

Text: Then one day, the sun returns.
Miranda: Then the, one day the sun returns.

Miranda again substitutes one short function word for another, but as she starts to read on, she realizes that the word doesn't work with the evolving sentence, so she corrects it. This is a case where correction was a productive strategy. Is it best for readers to correct all their miscues if they catch them? Efficiency suggests not. Often readers overcorrect (that is, they correct miscues that make sense and don't change the meaning), but often they don't even notice this kind of miscue.

Some Graphic Similarity, Correction Attempted

Text: Yet each and every creature . . .
Miranda: Yet each and every character . . .

Miranda's miscue of *character* for *creature* worked reasonably well in the meaning context of this sentence, but she nonetheless tried (unsuccessfully) to correct it, probably because she realized that it wasn't the word that was on the page. The word *creature* isn't particularly easy to decipher using phonics; if you recall the related word *create*, you might be inclined to read the *ea* digraph as two separate vowel sounds, and the *t* is pronounced as /t/. This would be an easy word to give up trying to pronounce if you didn't recognize it and the context didn't make it clear. (And although we can surmise that Miranda probably had the word in her vocabulary but just didn't recognize it, as far as she knew, it might have been a word that she didn't know at all. (If the word had been *chimera*, for instance, we wouldn't be at all surprised that it gave her trouble.)

In general, then, looking at Miranda's miscues that weren't a close graphic match, we don't see any particular signs of weakness as a reader. Although phonics didn't play a big role in these miscues, either it didn't need to (the miscue made sense or she corrected it) or it couldn't (she unsuccessfully tried to figure out *creature* after miscueing on it). If a word doesn't "fall into place" quickly, we can't necessarily determine it through phonics, particularly if we don't know whether the word is familiar to us or not. (We can misread a word for years even though it's a word we know. Did you ever read *misled* as "mizeled"? How long before you knew that the word seen in print as *victuals* is the same word, meaning food, that's pronounced "vittles"?)

Miscues with High Graphic Similarity

A number of Miranda's miscues were very close graphically to the word in the text, showing a good use of phonics, but some of these produced acceptable readings and some didn't. An important pattern to watch for in a struggling reader is miscues where she sounds out to the best of her ability, doesn't succeed, yet sticks with a miscue that doesn't make sense rather than using other strategies.

High Graphic Similarity, Semantically Acceptable

Text: . . . landing on every animal . . .
Miranda: . . . laying on every animal . . .

This section of text, which was about mosquitoes (a word that Miranda had been unable to read), accompanied a picture of a musk-ox covered with bugs. Especially given that additional piece of information, Miranda's miscue is a reasonable one and was probably unintentional in the sense that she didn't know she was making it.

High Graphic Similarity, Semantically Acceptable

> Text: . . . at last it is spring.
> Miranda: . . . at least it is spring.

This is a wonderful example of a miscue that differs only slightly from the word in the text and that also makes sense (although it changes the meaning very slightly). Readers often don't realize they're making a miscue like this one; it's graphically similar to what they see on the page, and it doesn't disrupt the flow of language and meaning. Trying to eliminate miscues like this one would slow down the reading process appreciably. Also, a miscue like this one doesn't mean that a reader needs work on short versus long vowels, since the miscue is meaning-driven and could be made by a proficient reader.

High Graphic Similarity, Semantically Acceptable, Corrected

> Text: Tens of caribou . . .
> Miranda: Tons, tens of caribou . . .

Like some of Miranda's other miscues, this one reflects the way readers often produce their own language rather than book language. The picture that accompanies this text looks like "tons of caribou," and "tens of caribou" is an unusual phrasing. Miranda's self-correction may have been prompted (as many self-corrections are) by realizing that the word she saw isn't quite what she said, or by seeing that the text ahead goes on to say, "hundreds of caribou, thousands of caribou."

High Graphic Similarity, Syntactically and Semantically Unacceptable, Slight Meaning Change

> Text: Polar bears wander across the frozen sea.
> Miranda: Polar bears wonder across the frozen sea.

Miranda's miscue of *wonder* for *wander* is only off by one letter and is as close as you can get phonetically without getting the word right. Vowels tend to be spelled differently after *w*; her short *u* (ʌ) here is the same one we hear in *was*. Miranda's problem wasn't with phonics but with not catching that her miscue didn't make sense (although it does evoke a charming image of pensive polar bears!). Miranda made several miscues of this type, suggesting that if anything she overused phonics to the detriment of creating a meaningful reading (although in this case it's possible that *wonder* was her pronunciation of *wander*, since the two words are homophones for some people).

High Graphic Similarity, Syntactically and Semantically Unacceptable

> Text: Musk-oxen form a protective circle around their young.
> Miranda: Musk-oxen from a protective circle around their young.

This miscue is also extremely close graphically, since it has all the right letters but in the wrong order. (Since *from* is a more common word than *form*, this substitution is more likely than the reverse, just as readers are more likely to read *was* for *saw* than vice versa.) However, this is a weaker miscue than *wonder* for *wander*, because it produces a sentence that isn't grammatical (the verb is eliminated). This miscue is also a sign of Miranda's occasional tendency to keep going even if what she reads doesn't make sense.

High Graphic Similarity, Known Word, Nonword Produced

> Text: Polygon-shaped mirrors of water . . .
> Miranda: $Polgon-shaped mirrors of water . . . (Dollar signs are used in miscue analysis to represent nonwords.)

Although *polygon* isn't a common word, Miranda knew it because her class had been studying the concept in math. It isn't surprising that she miscues on it in this context, however, because she was used to applying it to abstract, perfectly formed geometrical shapes on a piece of paper rather than to features of the natural world. Here the word is being used somewhat metaphorically—the water in the accompanying picture does exhibit polygon shapes, but they are approximate rather than precise and are further distorted by the viewing angle of the camera. Presumably Miranda uses phonics to come up with a reasonably close approximation of the word, but she doesn't make the semantic connection to a word she knows.

High Graphic Similarity, Unknown Word, Nonword Produced

> Text: white winter plumage
> Miranda: white winter $plummage

Miranda almost certainly doesn't know the word *plumage*, and again produces a miscue that uses phonics well (perhaps by analogy to *plum*). When she and I discussed this miscue after she had finished reading, she didn't change her pronunciation but was able to figure out from the accompanying photograph that the word referred to the bird's coat. This miscue is similar to those often made by proficient adult readers when they encounter a word that's not part of their oral vocabulary: they focus mainly on understanding what the word means from context and coming up with a good pronunciation that may or may not be the right one.

High Graphic Similarity, Known Word, Nonword Produced

> Text: Millions of mosquitoes swarm . . .
> Miranda: Millions of $moscouts swarm . . .

I've saved my favorite miscue for last. Miranda makes a good attempt on *mosquitoes* but doesn't come up with a real word. After she finished reading, we went back to that page in the book and discussed it at length; I wanted to see what it would take for her to figure out that this was a word she knew. I've transcribed our entire conversation about this miscue, during which she uses the photographs and other context and her knowledge of phonics to create meaning.

Although it takes Miranda longer to make the connection than it might take some other children, the process she goes through is the same: how do I reconcile the letters I see in print with what I know about the meaning of the text? Note the role I played in encouraging her to use varied information sources and reflect on possible strategies.

Sandra: Tell me how you knew it was bugs [*this has come up a bit earlier in the conversation*] from the reading even though you didn't know that word.

Miranda: They were all over the animals.

S: So I guess between the sentence and the picture . . .

M: How could animals stand that?

S: I know. Ew. And you know, if you were there, they'd probably land on you because humans are animals too . . . Take one more look at this word and think about the picture.

M: It looks like it says *toes.*

S: Toes, yes, that's part of the word. Any idea what that word might be from thinking about bugs, looking at the word, and looking at the picture?

M: Mos. Quit. Toes. Mos-quit-toes?

S: Does that sound like anything you've ever heard of?

M: No.

S: No. So . . . I'll give you a hint, it is something you've heard of. Any idea of what that could be? What are some kinds of bugs that could land on animals?

M: Mosquito. A tick. Ladybug . . . um . . . spider.

S: Look back at the word now, thinking about those kinds of bugs you just said. Ladybug, tick, mosquito, spider. Any of those fit? (*Miranda shakes head no*) You sure? Is it *ladybug*?

M: No.

S: How do you know?

M: Because it doesn't say ladybug.

S: Okay. Is it *tick*?

M: Could be. But I don't think so.

S: And why not, probably?

M: Because you can't see ticks that good.

S: But what about the word? Does the word look like it could be tick?

M: No.

S: Okay, why not?

M: Because it doesn't.

S: Okay. Mosquitoes.

M: Ohhhhhh. Mosquitoes.

Both (*Laughing*): Ahhhh!

S: And how was it that you realized?

M: Because I kind of looked at the *e-s* and then I kind of looked [at the picture].

S: Yes, and remember before when you were trying to figure out and you were saying mos-quit-toes? You were really close! Does that suggest . . .

M: Those don't look like mosquitoes.

S: You're right, they don't. Maybe they're just really small ones. Does that suggest to you anything about what to do when there's a particularly long word that you're stuck on?

M: If you know it's a bug or you know it's an animal or something, you can name some.

S: Right. And then look at it and see if it makes sense. Now when you first said spider, tick, mosquito, ladybug, you looked at this and said no, it's not any of those. Why do you think it was that you didn't realize that that was *mosquitoes*?

M: Because . . . 'cause I didn't think *mosquitoes* was spelled that long.

S: Oh! I bet if I had asked you to spell mosquito you would have had something like *m o s k* . . .

M: Probably.

What This All Means—for Miranda,
for Readers, and for Teachers

I gave a brief presentation on miscue analysis to the teachers at Miranda's school, many of whom had worked with her over the years as classroom and Title I teachers. (She wasn't a seriously troubled reader, merely one of many students who need extra support with literacy.) After I had showed them the entire picture-book text with all the miscues, summarized Miranda's retelling of what she'd read (which was adequate, including a few main ideas and a number of specific details), and played parts of the videotape of her listening to and discussing her miscues, we talked about what the teachers noticed.

Although many of them had previously assumed that children who are having problems with reading need more work on phonics, they admitted that Miranda's use of phonics was not deficient; even on very difficult words, she was able to come up with a guess that used a remarkable amount of the graphic information. (For instance, for *pasqueflowers*, she came up with "packwicky flowers, something like that," and for *ptarmigan* she tried "part-im-gan" and "perigan," obviously confused by the unusual *pt* digraph.) My assessment of Miranda was that she had a number of good reading strategies (although she wasn't developmentally as far along as one would like for fifth grade), but that she could use some coaching about noticing when what you've read doesn't make sense.

In a large-scale miscue analysis research study, Ken and Yetta Goodman discovered that there was never a single phonics rule or relationship that consistently caused a problem for any single child (Yetta Goodman, personal communication, 1996, referring to Goodman and Goodman, 1978). When we look at readers for whom reading is a challenge, their use of phonics typically places them in one of four broadly defined groups, which are really about their general development and strategies as readers:

1. They aren't really reading yet and need the kinds of support in becoming a reader that are discussed in Chapter 3.
2. They use phonics reasonably well as one of the cueing systems of written language, but either (like Miranda) need to be encouraged to focus a bit more on meaning as they read, or are lagging behind other children their age but would look like perfectly good readers if they were a few years younger.
3. They overuse phonics and word recognition to the extent that they appear to focus on a single word at a time, as if they were reading a list, rather than constructing meaningful text.

4. They overrely on prediction, context, and picture cues without enough attention to the text on the page.

Although children may be assigned a variety of labels by schools if they aren't succeeding as readers, and emotional factors such as a feeling of failure as a reader are an important part of the picture, these four categories can be very useful in deciding what to focus on with them.

None of these four groups of readers needs extensive drill on specific graphophonic relationships: some readers merely need to get better at integrating this knowledge the way mature readers do; all of them need to read, read, read, since that is the main way one becomes a better reader. Phonics needs to fall into place as a small, largely unconscious piece of the knowledge that literate people use.

Epilogue:
Where Do I Go from Here?

When I'd finished writing the first draft of this book, my editor, Toby Gordon, told me that I needed to add a conclusion. She said, "You need to tell your readers how to use what they've gained from this book." The following suggestions, listed in no particular order, contain ideas about how you can apply what you've learned and keep your knowledge about phonics fresh in your mind:

1. Pay attention to your own use of phonics when you read and write. When you come to an unfamiliar word, note how you use your knowledge of sound/letter relationships. What other knowledge do you use? When you go to write a word that you aren't quite sure how to spell, how much do you depend on spelling rules? How much do you use other knowledge, such as analogies to other words or your memory of what the word looks like? How does all of this relate to the strategies you might help students develop?
2. Particularly if you work with young children, try taking a child's story and rewriting the piece phonetically, using the symbols from the appendix. Then look at the child's spellings and see what features of his or her inventions represent the phonetics of the words.
3. Put into your own words some of what you've learned from this book, and then share this knowledge with parents in a newsletter, discussions, or a presentation.

4. Use reading and writing conferences with children to explore their knowledge of the grapho-phonic system. For instance, one week during reading conferences with your students, you may want to notice the extent to which each of them uses "sounding out" as a strategy for unfamiliar words, and how successfully each does so. In conferencing about children's writing, you could ask each child to tell you how he or she came up with a particular invented spelling.

5. When you see discussions of phonics in the public media, try to mentally formulate responses to statements such as the following:

> Take reading. You and I and just about everyone else learned to read by the phonics method. First we learned our ABCs, then we learned to match sounds with letters, and soon we could write simple sentences. . . . Phonics isn't fancy or intricate. But it works, and has for hundreds of years. (Bob Dole, 1996, from a campaign speech)

If you feel so moved, write a letter to the editor about a discussion of phonics or spelling you've seen in the newspaper.

6. If your school is considering adopting textbooks with an extensive focus on phonics or spelling, use the knowledge you've gained from this book to evaluate and critique what you see. If such textbooks are mandated and you aren't happy with what they contain, work with other teachers to communicate your critiques to those in power.

7. Read one or more of the books or articles I've cited to deepen your knowledge in particular areas.

8. Write to me and share some thoughts about what you've learned, lingering questions, or ideas you're trying out in your classroom. I can be reached through Heinemann or by e-mail at sandra@ed.pdx.edu

Finally, /hæpē fonɪks/ and GUD LUK WF ENVETD SPELIG! (If you can read those, you've passed the final!)

Appendix:
Phonetic Symbols Used in This Book

	Symbol used here	Word containing the sound	IPA symbol
CONSONANTS			
voiced bilabial stop	/b/	big	/b/
unvoiced bilabial stop	/p/	pig	/p/
voiced alveolar stop	/d/	dip	/d/
unvoiced alveolar stop	/t/	tip	/t/
voiced velar stop	/g/	god	/g/
unvoiced velar stop	/k/	cod	/k/
glottal stop	/ʔ/	middle of *uh-oh*; bo*tt*le in some versions of English	/ʔ/
voiced labiodental fricative	/v/	*v*an	/v/
unvoiced labiodental fricative	/f/	*f*an	/f/
voiced dental fricative	/ð/	*th*y	/ð/
unvoiced dental fricative	/θ/	*th*igh	/θ/
voiced alveolar fricative	/z/	*z*ip	/z/

unvoiced alveolar fricative	/s/	sip	/s/
voiced palatal fricative	/ž/	azure	/ž/ or /ʒ/
unvoiced palatal fricative	/š/	ship	/š/ or /ʃ/
voiced palatal affricate	/ǰ/	jar	/ǰ/ or /dž/
unvoiced palatal affricate	/č/	char	/č/ or /tʃ/
bilabial nasal	/m/	map	/m/
alveolar nasal	/n/	nap	/n/
velar nasal	/ŋ/	sing	/ŋ/
liquid	/l/	lap	/l/
liquid	/r/	rap	/r/ or /ɹ/
glide	/w/	wet	/w/
glide	/y/	yet	/y/ or /j/
glide	/h/	hit	/h/
VOWELS			
high front tense	/ē/	beat	/i/
high front lax	/ɪ/	bit	/ɪ/
mid front tense	/ā/	bait	/e/
mid front lax	/ɛ/	bet	/ɛ/
low front lax	/æ/	bat	/æ/
mid central unstressed (schwa)	/ə/	about	/ə/
mid central unstressed rounded (schwar)	/ɚ/	father	/ɚ/or /əɹ/
low central lax	/ʌ/	but	/ʌ/
high back tense rounded	/u/	boot	/u/
high back lax rounded	/ʊ/	book	/ʊ/
mid back tense rounded	/ō/	boat	/o/

mid back lax rounded	/ɔ/	bought	/ɔ/
low back lax rounded	/o/	hot	/ɒ/
diphthong (central to front)	/ɪ/	high	/ɒɪ/
diphthong (central to back)	/au/	how	/ɒu/
diphthong (back to front)	/ɔi/	boy	/ɔɪ/

References

Adams, Marilyn. 1990. *Beginning to read: Thinking and learning about print.* Cambridge, MA: The MIT Press.

Anderson, Richard C., Elfrieda H. Hiebert, Judith A. Scott, and Ian A. Wilkinson. 1984. *Becoming a nation of readers: The report of the Commission on Reading.* Washington: National Institute of Education.

Andersson, Lars-Gunnar, and Peter Trudgill. 1990. *Bad language.* New York: Penguin.

Avery, Carol. 1993. *. . . And with a light touch: Learning about reading, writing, and teaching with first graders.* Portsmouth, NH: Heinemann.

Bissex, Glenda. 1980. *Gnys at wrk: A child learns to read and write.* Cambridge, MA: Harvard.

Brengleman, Frederick H. 1970. Dialect and the teaching of spelling. *Research in the teaching of English* 4:129–138.

Chomsky, Carol. 1971. Write first, read later. *Childhood Education* 47:296–299.

Clay, Marie M. 1975. *What did I write?: Beginning writing behaviour.* Portsmouth, NH: Heinemann.

———. 1979. *The early detection of reading difficulties: A diagnostic survey with recovery procedures.* Portsmouth, NH: Heinemann.

Clymer, Theodore. 1963. The utility of phonic generalizations in the primary grades. *The Reading Teacher* 16:252–258.

Cummings, D. W. 1988. *American English spelling: An informal description.* Baltimore: Johns Hopkins.

Dahl, Karin L., and Penny Freppon. 1995. A comparison of inner city children's interpretations of reading and writing instruction in the early grades in skill-based and whole language classrooms. *Reading Research Quarterly* 30:50–74.

DeFord, Diane. 1985. Validating the construct of theoretical orientation in reading instruction. *Reading Research Quarterly* 20:351–367.

DeFord, Diane, Carol A. Lyons, and Gay S. Pinnell. Eds. 1991. *Bridges to literacy: Learning from reading recovery.* Portsmouth, NH: Heinemann.

Delpit, Lisa. 1995. *Other people's children: Cultural conflict in the classroom.* New York: The New Press.

Dillard, J. L. 1972. *Black English: Its history and usage in the United States.* New York: Random House.

Dole, Bob. 1996. Campaign Speech, De La Salle High School, Minneapolis, July 17.

Durkin, Dolores. 1978–1979. What classroom observations reveal about reading comprehension instruction. *Reading Research Quarterly* 4:481–533.

Durr, William K. 1986. *Adventures (Level G of Houghton Mifflin reading): Teacher's guide.* Boston: Houghton Mifflin.

Edelsky, Carole. 1986. *Writing in a bilingual program: Había una vez.* Norwood, NJ: Ablex.

Edelsky, Carole, Bess Altwerger, and Barbara Flores. 1990. *Whole language: What's the difference?* Portsmouth, NH: Heinemann.

Fisher, Bobbi. 1991. *Joyful learning: A whole language kindergarten.* Portsmouth, NH: Heinemann.

———. 1995. *Thinking and learning together: Curriculum and community in a primary classroom.* Portsmouth, NH: Heinemann.

Fisher, Carol J., and Catherine E. Studier. 1977. *Misspellings of children in the middle grades* (Studies in Language Education, Report No. 29). Athens, GA: Department of Language Education, University of Georgia. (ERIC Document Reproduction Service Document ED 143 030.)

Fitzsimmons, Robert J., and Bradley M. Loomer. 1978. *Spelling: Learning and instruction—research and practice.* Ames, IA: Iowa State Department of Public Instruction and the University of Iowa.

Freeman, David E., and Yvonne S. Freeman. 1992. *Whole language for second language learners.* Portsmouth, NH: Heinemann.

———. 1994. *Between worlds: Access to second language acquisition.* Portsmouth, NH: Heinemann.

———. 1997. *Teaching reading and writing in Spanish in the bilingual classroom.* Portsmouth, NH: Heinemann.

References

Fromkin, Victoria, and Robert Rodman. 1993. *An introduction to language*. 5th ed. Fort Worth: Harcourt Brace Jovanovich.

Gadsden, Vivian L., and Daniel A. Wagner. Eds. 1995. *Literacy among African American youth: Issues in learning, teaching, and schooling*. Cresskill, NJ: Hampton Press.

Goodman, Ken. 1993. *Phonics phacts*. Portsmouth, NH: Heinemann.

———. 1996. *On reading*. Portsmouth, NH: Heinemann.

Goodman, Kenneth S., and Catherine Buck. 1973. Dialect barriers to reading comprehension: Revisited. *The Reading Teacher* 27:6–12.

Goodman, Kenneth S., and Fred Gollasch. 1980. Word omissions: Deliberate and non-deliberate. *Reading Research Quarterly* 16:6–31.

Goodman, Kenneth S., and Yetta Goodman. 1978. *Reading of American children whose language is a stable rural dialect of English or a language other than English* (Research Report No. NIE-C-00-3-0087, U.S. Department of Health Education and Welfare). Tucson: Program in Language and Literacy, University of Arizona.

Goodman, Kenneth S., Yetta M. Goodman, and Wendy J. Hood. Eds. 1989. *The whole language evaluation book*. Portsmouth, NH: Heinemann.

Goodman, Kenneth S., Patrick Shannon, Yvonne S. Freeman, and Sharon Murphy. 1988. *Report card on basal readers*. Katonah, NY: Richard C. Owen.

Goodman, Yetta M., Dorothy J. Watson, and Carolyn L. Burke. 1987. *Reading miscue inventory: Alternative procedures*. Katonah, NY: Richard C. Owen.

Graves, Bill. 1996. Spellbound for the summer. *The (Portland) Oregonian*. July 21:B1,B7.

Harste, Jerome C., and Carolyn L. Burke. 1980. Examining instructional assumptions: The child as informant. *Theory into Practice* 19:170–178.

Haussler, Myna. 1984. *Transitions into literacy: A working paper*. Occasional paper No. 10. Tucson, AZ: Program in Language and Literacy, College of Education, University of Arizona.

Holmes, Steven A. 1996. Black voice of the streets is defended and criticized. *New York Times* (national ed.) December 30, p. A7.

Horn, Ernest. 1929. The child's early experience with the letter *a*. *Journal of Educational Psychology* 20:161–168.

Horvath, Barbara M. 1985. Variation in Australian English: The sociolects of Sydney. Cambridge: Cambridge University Press.

Juel, Connie, Priscilla L. Griffith, and Philip B. Gough. 1986. Acquisition of literacy: A longitudinal study of children in first and second grade. *Journal of Educational Psychology* 78: 243–255.

Krashen, Steven D. 1993. *The power of reading.* Englewood, CO: Libraries Unlimited.

Kreidler, Charles W. 1989. *The pronunciation of English.* New York: Basil Blackwell.

Labov, William. 1969. The logic of nonstandard English. *Georgetown Monographs on Language and Linguistics* 22:1–31.

Ladefoged, Peter. 1982. *A course in phonetics.* 2d ed. San Diego: Harcourt Brace Jovanovich.

Lakoff, George, and Mark Johnson. 1980. *Metaphors we live by.* Chicago: University of Chicago.

Leap, William L. 1993. *American Indian English.* Salt Lake City: University of Utah Press.

Manning, Maryann, Gary Manning, and Roberta Long. 1989. *Effects of a whole language and skills-oriented program on the literacy development of inner city primary children.* Paper presented at the Annual Meeting of the Mid-South Educational Research Association New Orleans, Nov. 8–10. (ERIC Document Reproduction Service Document ED 324 642.)

————. 1990. *Writing development of inner city primary students: Comparative effects of a whole language and skills-oriented program.* Paper presented at the Annual Meeting of the Mid-South Educational Research Association New Orleans, Nov. 14-16. (ERIC Document Reproduction Service Document ED 336 745.)

McGee, Lea M., and Donald J. Richgels. 1989. "K is Kristen's": Learning the alphabet from a child's perspective. *The Reading Teacher* 43:216–225.

Mills, Heidi, Timothy O'Keefe, and Diane Stephens. 1992. *Looking closely: Exploring the role of phonics in one whole language classroom.* Urbana, IL: National Council of Teachers of English.

Moustafa, Margaret. 1993. Recoding in whole language reading instruction. *Language Arts* 70:483–487.

————. 1995. Children's productive phonological recoding. *Reading Research Quarterly* 30:464–476.

Nagy, William E., Patricia A. Herman, and Richard C. Anderson. 1985. Learning words from context. *Reading Research Quarterly* 20: 233–253.

Pandell, Karen. 1993. *Land of dark, land of light: The Arctic National Wildlife Refuge*. New York: Dutton.

Pinker, Steven. 1994. *The language instinct: How the mind creates language*. New York: Morrow.

Pinnell, Gay S. 1989. Reading recovery: Helping at-risk children learn to read. *Elementary School Journal* 90:161–183.

Read, Charles. 1971. Pre-school children's knowledge of English phonology. *Harvard Educational Review* 41:1–34.

———. 1975. *Children's categorizations of speech sounds in English*. Research Report No. 17. Urbana, IL: National Council of Teachers of English.

Read, Charles, Zhang Yun-Fei, Nie Hong-Kin, and Ding Bao-Qing. 1986. The ability to manipulate speech sounds depends on knowing alphabetic writing. *Cognition, 24,* 31–44.

Rhodes, Lynn. 1981. I can read! Predictable books as resources for reading and writing instruction. *Reading Teacher* 34:511–518.

Rosenblatt, Louise M. 1978. *The reader, the text, the poem*. Carbondale, IL: Southern Illinois University Press.

Routman, Regie. 1996. *Literacy at the crossroads: Crucial talk about reading, writing, and other teaching dilemmas*. Portsmouth, NH: Heinemann.

Smith, Frank. 1982. *Writing and the writer*. New York: Holt, Rinehart and Winston.

———. 1988a. *Joining the literacy club*. Portsmouth, NH: Heinemann.

———. 1988b. *Understanding reading*. 4th ed. Hillsdale, NJ: Lawrence Erlbaum.

Smitherman, Geneva. 1977. *Talkin and testifyin: The language of Black America*. Detroit: Wayne State University Press.

———. 1994. *Black talk*. Boston: Houghton Mifflin.

Stetson, Elton G., and Frances Boutin. 1980. *Spelling instruction: Diagnostic-prescriptive minus the diagnostic*. Unpublished paper. (ERIC Document Reproduction Service No. ED 205 980.)

Treiman, Rebecca. 1993. *Beginning to spell*. New York: Oxford.

Turner, Richard L. 1989. The "great" debate—can both Carbo and Chall be right? *Phi Delta Kappan* 71:276–283.

Venezky, Richard L. 1970. *The structure of English orthography*. The Hague: Mouton.

Weaver, Constance. 1988. *Reading process and practice*. Portsmouth, NH: Heinemann.

————. 1990. *Understanding whole language: From principles to practice.* Portsmouth, NH: Heinemann.

Wells, Gordon. 1986. *The meaning makers: Children learning language and using language to learn.* Portsmouth, NH: Heinemann.

Wilde, Sandra. 1987. An analysis of the development of spelling and punctuation in selected third- and fourth-grade children. Doctoral dissertation, University of Arizona, 1986. *Dissertation Abstracts International* 47:2452A.

————. 1989a. "Looking at invented spelling: A kid-watcher's guide to spelling, part 1." In Kenneth S. Goodman, Yetta M. Goodman, and Wendy Hood, eds. *The Whole Language Evaluation Book*, 213–226. Portsmouth, NH: Heinemann.

————. 1989b. "Understanding spelling strategies: A kid-watcher's guide to spelling, part 2." In Kenneth Goodman, Yetta Goodman, and Wendy Hood, eds. *The Whole Language Evaluation Book*, 227–236. Portsmouth, NH: Heinemann.

————. 1990. Spelling textbooks: A critical review. *Linguistics and Education* 2:259–280.

————. 1992. *You kan red this! Spelling and punctuation for whole language classrooms*, K–6. Portsmouth, NH: Heinemann.

Wolfram, Walt. 1991. *Dialects and American English.* Englewood Cliffs, NJ: Prentice Hall.

Wolfram, Walt, and Donna Christian. 1989. *Dialects and education: Issues and answers.* Englewood Cliffs, NJ: Prentice Hall Regents.

Index

_____

(Page numbers for definitions are in italics.)

Index